Tamasin Day-Lewis

food YOU CAN'T SAY NO TO

Tamasin Day-Lewis

food YOU CAN'T SAY NO TO

PHOTOGRAPHY BY SIMON WHEELER

Quadrille
PUBLISHING

NOTES

- Use fresh herbs, sea salt and freshly ground black pepper unless otherwise suggested.
- Use large eggs, organic or at least free-range. Anyone who is pregnant or in a vulnerable health group should avoid recipes that use raw egg whites or lightly cooked eggs.
- Use unwaxed citrus fruit, especially if you are using the zest.
- Timings are for conventional ovens. If using a fan-assisted oven, reduce the temperature by 15°C (1 Gas mark). Use an oven thermometer to check the temperature.

Publishing director **Jane O'Shea**
Creative director **Helen Lewis**
Art direction & design **Lucy Gowans**
Photographer **Simon Wheeler**
Production **Aysun Hughes, Vincent Smith**

First published in 2012 by
Quadrille Publishing Limited
Alhambra House
27–31 Charing Cross Road
London WC2H 0LS
www.quadrille.co.uk

This edition produced for The Book People,
Hall Wood Avenue, Haydock, St Helens,
WA11 9UL

Cataloguing in Publication Data: a catalogue record for this book is available from the British Library.

ISBN 978 184949 163 1

Printed in China

CONTENTS

What do you think of when you think of food you can't say *no* to? It's very often the simplest of things like home made bread still yeasty-warm from the oven, spread with lashings of butter. Or a dish linked indelibly to your childhood like roast chicken on Sunday.

The simpler, is, so often, the better.

Here is a book filled with good things, some of which you will find familiar but different, like this nearly-but-not crumble: a rhubarb and strawberry crisp with toasted oats and hazelnuts, or Coronation Crab, a dish as sleekly well-tuned and fitting as its alma mater, Coronation Chicken.

Other dishes will, I hope, surprise and delight with their elegant, yet unencumbered simplicity; with a few good ingredients, or a witty new take on an old and tried and tested. My salmon and scallop chowder is more of a fully fledged stew than a soup, smoky with bacon, oily with chunks of wild salmon and flecked with a little tarragon. Or try the simple, starchy pleasure of gnocchi dressed to kill with asparagus, tomatoes, green olives and mascarpone. A beauty of a dish.

We can never resist summer berries in this house; I mix strawberries and raspberries from the fruit cage with a few of my rare, Alpine-like tiny white strawberries and some bought-in cherries and blueberries, but make your own mélange, the berries soaked and bled into a Cassis syrup and piled high on mascarpone cream and the lightest of genoise sponges. Celebratory.

There are some things we can **never** say *no* to; after all, we are all small children at heart. It's a question of always keeping a proper store-cupboard, freezer and fridge so that even in extremis you can conjure a treat out of almost nowhere. Grandmother's tart, -torta della nonna- is one such, that the Italians make as many versions of as there are grandmothers; it's about using ingredients you almost always have, its vanilla and lemon-scented custard strewn with toasted pine nuts and grated bitter chocolate before you eat it chilled and straight from the fridge.

Remember the old-fashioned chocolate fridge cake you stirred when you were young, with bashed up digestives, lousy chocolate and too much golden syrup? My re-worked adult-rated version will, I hope, become an instant and instantly made delight in your kitchen with its dark chocolate, almonds, pistachios and jeweled with Morello cherries.

If you can say *no* to a pie avert your eyes now, but I never can, no more than I can stop tinkering with new pie recipes, be they sweet or savoury. Hot, warm or cold, in the kitchen, the garden or on the beach, my primavera pie with its verdant green vegetables, asparagus, broad beans, peas and artichokes, wrapped in a caul of prosciutto and a Parmesan custard is irresistible; and so is the blue cheese, celery, red onion and walnut pie.

Perhaps the one thing that binds all these dishes together is the fact that they are all home made from scratch. That they may stir the magic of memory, of childhood, and are often simply the things we know and love best made a little more sophisticated. These are dishes that have heart but are not about wizardry, invention or kitchen pyrotechnics. This, I hope, is a book filled with the food we **really** can't say *no* to.

SIMPLE SPECIAL THINGS

What makes something simple, special? I think it's all about the unexpected, about knowing how to surprise and dazzle with a detail.

My hot Greek, for example, is a classic Greek salad: salty feta, glossy olives, tomatoes, mint and oregano, bound with a little yoghurt and baked in a filo parcel.

Home-made rolls are flecked with caraway and fennel seeds. Press a hot, marmalade-coated sausage into one of them and you have about as heavenly a conjunction as you can imagine – for breakfast, brunch, lunch or a midnight feast.

I have long loved the pizza's classier cousin, the pissaladière. The trick is all in the layering. Salt with sweet, piquant with lactic. My best yet has tongues of roasted aubergine lolling on red onions, cooked to near oblivion, with lines of anchovies, a few olives and last-minute spoonfuls of stracchino that don't get time to melt.

Yalla Yalla chicken livers are Beirut street food at its best. Cooked quickly with garlic, lemon and a sticky splosh of fruity molasses, this gem of a dish – bejewelled with pomegranate seeds – assaults the palate and seduces instantly.

Colour is, to the eye, as important a sense as taste is to the tongue. Look at the brazen, vermilion red of the purée of peppers strewn with black olives, mint and walnuts. It can stand alone or hold its own with a couple more mezze, whose colours and textures are defined by their simple beauty and verdancy. That is what this chapter is all about: rawness, simplicity and colour – and the heights to which they can reach, effortlessly.

The home kitchen, I believe, is not the place to intimidate, it is the place to comfort and restore, to sustain and nourish. Where all should appear artless. Where the simple is made special, easily.

A CLUTCH OF EASY MEZZE

'Mezze' from the Persian '*mzzz*' means bite relish. Mezze are eaten – relished – all over The Balkans, Turkey, Greece, Egypt, Morocco and in the Lebanon, where they are second to none. Mezze are, like tapas, dishes to eat while drinking and gossiping and, as we all know, a drink or gossip shared is the best way. (*Also illustrated on previous pages*)

OLIVE & PARSLEY SALAD

Simple, clean flavours give this salad its unusual piquant, sweet spiciness. Best made with the giant emerald-green Mammuth olives if you can track them down.

serves 4 as part of a mezze spread

200g large green olives
1 small red onion, peeled and finely chopped
1 small carrot, peeled and grated
1 tsp cumin seeds
⅓ tsp cayenne pepper
2 tbsp finely chopped flat-leaf parsley
1 tbsp fruity olive oil
1 tbsp pomegranate molasses

Halve and pit the olives and mix with the onion and carrot in a serving dish. Toast the cumin seeds in a hot, dry frying pan for a minute or so until fragrant, then crush using a pestle and mortar. Add to the salad with the cayenne, parsley, olive oil and pomegranate molasses. Mix everything together with your hands and allow the salad to stand for 10 minutes before serving.

RED PEPPER SALAD WITH OLIVES & WALNUTS

This vibrant, vermilion purée is good served with warm pitta, toast or leaves of red or white chicory.

serves 4 as part of a mezze spread

6 Romano or other red peppers
1 tbsp pomegranate molasses
sea salt
10–12 black olives, pitted and halved
1 tbsp walnuts, chopped
splash of fruity olive oil
1 tsp chopped mint
handful of torn basil leaves

Grill the peppers or scorch by turning on a fork over a gas flame, until charred on all sides. Put in a bowl, cover with cling film and leave for 20 minutes. Peel away the skins and remove the seeds from the peppers, then put into a blender along with their juices and blitz to a smooth purée.

Transfer the red pepper purée to a serving bowl, stir in the pomegranate molasses and season with a little salt. Scatter the olives and chopped walnuts over the top, dress with the olive oil and finish with the herbs.

MUHAMMARA

Muhammara or 'made red' is a lovely coarse-textured, creamy paste of spiced walnuts, breadcrumbs and roasted peppers, sharpened and intensified with lemony pomegranate molasses and a little yoghurt. The cayenne kicks in according to your taste, so judge accordingly. Serve muhammara on scoops of lettuce, toasted pitta bread or oat cakes.

serves 4 as part of a mezze spread

2 Romano or other red peppers
3 heaped tbsp day-old wholemeal breadcrumbs
½–1 tsp cayenne pepper, to taste
150ml boiling water
1 tbsp pine nuts
1–1½ tsp cumin seeds
150g walnuts
½ tbsp pomegranate molasses
sea salt and black pepper

Grill the peppers or scorch by turning on a fork over a gas flame, until charred on all sides. Put in a bowl, cover with cling film and leave for 20 minutes. Peel away the skins and remove the seeds from the peppers, then put into a blender or food processor, adding any juices, and blitz to a purée.

Tip the breadcrumbs into a bowl, sprinkle with ½ tsp cayenne and pour on the hot water. Stir and set aside for 10 minutes or so to let the breadcrumbs absorb the water.

Toast the pine nuts in a hot, dry frying pan, shaking the pan frequently, until the nuts begin to turn pale brown and look oily. Tip out onto a plate and set aside. Toast the cumin seeds in the pan for a minute or so until fragrant, then crush them using a pestle and mortar.

Add the breadcrumb mixture to the pepper purée in the blender or food processor with the walnuts, pomegranate molasses, toasted cumin and some salt and pepper. Process to a coarse paste, then taste and adjust the seasoning, adding a little more cayenne for extra heat if you wish. If the paste is a bit thick, add a little more hot water.

Transfer to a serving dish and scatter over the toasted pine nuts.

YALLA YALLA CHICKEN LIVERS

There's a little restaurant in London's Soho called Yalla Yalla ('quick, quick'), which serves wonderful Lebanese street food. It has taken many visits and many months to persuade Aga, the proprietress, to part with the recipe, but it was worth the wait. Aren't you lucky!

serves 2 as a starter;
4 as part of a mezze spread

200–220g organic/free-range chicken livers
1 tbsp olive oil
1 garlic clove, peeled and finely chopped
sea salt and black pepper
2 tbsp lemon juice
2 tbsp pomegranate molasses
1 heaped tbsp chopped parsley
2 tsp pomegranate seeds, extracted from a fresh pomegranate

Trim the chicken livers, removing the membranes and tubes, then cut into bite-sized pieces. Heat the olive oil in a frying pan, add the livers and cook over a brisk heat for 3–4 minutes, turning them gently once browned underneath. Add the garlic with a pinch each of salt and pepper and toss the livers. Add the lemon juice and pomegranate molasses and cook for another couple of minutes, turning occasionally, until the sauce reduces and thickens a little. The livers should be browned on the outside but still pink in the middle.

Remove from the heat, sprinkle over the chopped parsley and pomegranate seeds and serve.

AUBERGINES FATTEH

This is a pretty and substantial salad, the colours of the peppers and tomatoes, lettuce and parsley making it festive enough to grace any party.

serves 4–6 as part of a mezze spread

2 large aubergines
olive oil, for brushing
2 large tomatoes
1½ wholemeal pitta breads
1 tbsp pomegranate molasses
sea salt and black pepper
3 tbsp chopped flat-leaf parsley
1 small cucumber, or ½ standard one
1 garlic clove, peeled and crushed
450g live yoghurt, strained in a muslin-lined sieve for about an hour
1 red pepper, cored, deseeded and diced
2 Little Gem lettuces, quartered

Preheat the oven to 180°C/Gas 4. Cut the aubergines lengthways into slices, brush both sides with olive oil and lay on a large baking sheet. Roast in the oven until tender, about 20 minutes.

To peel the tomatoes, spike with the tip of a knife, then immerse in a bowl of boiling hot water for 30 seconds to loosen the skins. Immediately drain and refresh under cold water. Prise out the core with the tip of a small knife, then peel away the skin. Halve the tomatoes and scoop out the seeds, then cut the flesh into small cubes.

Brush both sides of the pitta breads generously with olive oil and either griddle or bake for a few minutes until crisp. Cut into small strips or squares.

While the aubergines are still warm, tip them into a bowl and pour over the pomegranate molasses. Sprinkle with a little salt and scatter over the chopped parsley. Toss to combine.

Peel the cucumber, halve lengthways and scoop out the seeds, then dice the flesh. Mix the crushed garlic into the strained yoghurt, then stir in the diced cucumber. Season with salt and pepper to taste.

Transfer the aubergines to a serving bowl and strew the pitta bread, diced pepper and tomatoes on top. Surround with the lettuce quarters and spoon the yoghurt and cucumber over before serving.

BROAD BEANS WITH DILL & YOGHURT

You may serve this dish with lamb as an accompaniment, or as it is here, with a heap of exotic, vibrant-hued other mezze.

serves 4 as part of a mezze spread

1kg broad beans in pods
4 tbsp olive oil
2 medium onions, peeled and finely sliced
sea salt and black pepper
1 tsp sugar
juice of ½ lemon
3 tbsp finely chopped dill, plus a few extra leaves
1 large garlic clove, peeled and crushed
200g Greek yoghurt
few flat-leaf parsley leaves, torn

Pod the broad beans. Add to a pan of fast-boiling water and blanch for 3 minutes, then drain, reserving 75ml of the water. Refresh the beans under cold water, drain and slip them out of their skins.

Heat the olive oil in a frying pan and sauté the sliced onions with a pinch of salt to help them exude their juices. Once the onions have started to soften, stir in the sugar. Add the beans with their reserved cooking water and the lemon juice. Cover and simmer very gently for 30 minutes. Uncover, sprinkle over the chopped dill, then put the lid back on and leave to cool.

Stir the garlic into the yoghurt and season with salt and pepper to taste. Spoon into a serving dish and scatter over the parsley and a few dill leaves.

Tip the broad beans into a serving dish. Accompany with the yoghurt and some bread and black olives if you like.

SPICY AUBERGINES WITH WALNUTS & PARSLEY

This is a new way I've discovered with aubergines for when you feel you want a change from the baba ganoush route. It wowed everybody the first time I made it with its unexpected flavour and depth, its smoky softness and nutty texture.

serves 8 as part of a mezze spread

2 large aubergines
2 tsp za'tar (make your own, see below)
1 large garlic clove, peeled and crushed
2 tsp chopped mint leaves
1 tbsp lemon juice, or to taste
sea salt and black pepper
1 tbsp boiling water
a little good olive oil
1 tbsp finely chopped parsley
1 tbsp chopped walnuts
a knife tip of cayenne pepper

Prick the aubergines in a few places with the tip of a knife. Grill or hold with tongs over a gas flame, turning until charred all over and cooked through. This should take about 5 minutes, but test with a skewer. Once cool enough to handle, peel away the skin. Roughly mash the aubergines on a plate with a fork.

Put the za'tar, crushed garlic, mint, lemon juice and some seasoning into a mortar, add the boiling water and stir to mix. Stir in the aubergine, then taste and adjust the seasoning, adding a little more lemon juice if needed.

Transfer to a plate, add a libation of olive oil and sprinkle over the chopped parsley, walnuts and cayenne. Serve with hot strips of pitta or my fennel and caraway seed rolls (see page 26), split and toasted.

ZA'TAR

This is really a pick 'n' mix your own spice mix, to which you can add cumin, fennel, coriander seeds and oregano. I add za'tar to strained yoghurt, raita, Middle Eastern style salads and mezze dishes. I also sprinkle it onto pitta bread brushed with olive oil, and griddle to accompany mezze.

Toast 2 tbsp sesame seeds briefly in a hot, dry small frying pan until they jump and turn biscuit coloured. Tip into a bowl and stir in ¾ tbsp very finely chopped thyme leaves, 1½ tsp sumac and sea salt to taste. Store in a lidded jar.

HOT GREEK FILOS

This is a 5-minute wonder to prepare, followed by 20 minutes in a hot oven. I had the idea of wrapping up all those lovely flavours you find in a Greek salad and parcelling them into buttery-crisp filo leaves. I worried that the olives might overwhelm, but they didn't. I made two different styles, an envelope and a purse, and they both turned out equally gorgeous. Do not attempt to eat straight from the oven – they seem to retain heat like nothing on earth.

makes 4

10 leaves of filo (from a 250g packet feuilles de filo)
30g unsalted butter, melted, for brushing
1 tbsp sesame seeds
1 tbsp kalonji (nigella) seeds

for the filling
1 small courgette
10–12 cherry tomatoes, halved
100g (½ standard packet) Greek feta cheese
2 tsp chopped oregano leaves
12 small olives (optional), pitted and halved
1 heaped tbsp organic Greek bio yoghurt
1 heaped tsp tahini
1 small garlic clove, peeled and crushed
2 tsp chopped mint leaves
black pepper

Preheat the oven to 180°C/Gas 4. For the filling, using a swivel vegetable peeler, cut the courgette lengthways into long ribbons and place in a bowl with the halved tomatoes. Crumble in the feta in bite-sized pieces and add the oregano and olives, if using. Toss to mix.

For the dressing, stir the yoghurt, tahini, garlic and mint together in a small bowl. Tip the dressing onto the salad and scrunch over some pepper (no salt, the feta has it all). Turn to mix gently with a spoon.

Cut the filo sheets in half, to give 20 squares. To make envelope parcels, brush each filo square with butter and layer in 4 piles. Divide the filling between them, placing it in the centre and brush the surrounding filo with butter. Fold one side over, brush with butter, then fold the other side over. Fold the ends in to fashion an envelope and brush all over with butter.

To make purses, brush the filo squares with butter and assemble in 4 piles, but stagger the squares, to make star-pointed piles. Plonk a large spoonful of the filling in the centre of each pile, gather up the surrounding filo and scrunch into a purse. Brush with melted butter.

Place the filo packages on a baking sheet and sprinkle with the sesame and kalonji seeds. Bake for 20 minutes or until browned and crisp. Transfer to a wire rack and leave for 10 minutes before eating.

POSH BUBBLE

Smartening up everyday leftovers with an exceptional ingredient or two turns an economy dish into something luxurious. The Beaufort goo and the salty crisp prosciutto elevate cabbage and potato to brunch or lunch status. Indeed, I ate these bronzed bubble and squeak cakes without any extras for lunch. They are slightly sloppier than the standard version because of the molten cheese, but all the lighter for being flourless.

serves 1

1 large potato equivalent of cold mash (milked, buttered and seasoned in the usual way)
2 heaped tbsp cold, cooked, buttered shredded cabbage
about 50g Beaufort or Gruyère, coarsely grated
1 large slice prosciutto, torn
sea salt and black pepper
1 tbsp olive oil

Scrape the potato and cabbage onto a plate and mash together. Work the grated cheese into the potato cake with the masher, then mix in the torn prosciutto. Season with a little salt and pepper to taste. With your hands, shape the mixture into three rough cakes.

Heat the olive oil in a non-stick frying pan. When hot, slide in the bubble cakes and cook over a lively heat for 4–5 minutes. Flip the cakes over and cook for a further 4 minutes or so until golden brown. You will notice the cakes changing shape and filling the pan a little more as the cheese turns molten. You may wish to cook them for an extra couple of minutes on each side to colour them more.

Slide the cakes onto a warm plate and eat them just as they are.

RED SALAD

This is a lovely beginning-of-summer salad. I first made it in mid-May, its colour and bite reflecting the burgeoning mood of light and heat. The redness: crimson radish, purple-red onion, vermilion tomato and maroon rice are a painter's palette. You may omit the chilli, or the kalonji seeds, if you like, but they give the salad spirit – a sort of warm embrace.

You will need no further embellishment with this dish; the astringence, substance, nuttiness of the rice and piquancy of the dressing, turned into it while still hot, work a beautiful magic with the salt feta and radish crunch.

serves 2

120g Camargue red rice (preferably organic)
1 small red onion, peeled and finely sliced
1 small red chilli, deseeded and finely sliced (optional)
12 radishes, trimmed and thinly sliced
12 cherry tomatoes, halved
1 small fennel bulb
handful of flat-leaf parsley, chopped
handful of mint leaves, chopped
2–3 spring onions, trimmed and thinly sliced
70g (about ⅓ packet) feta
1 tsp kalonji (nigella) seeds (optional)
1 tbsp pine nuts

for the dressing
1 garlic clove (ideally new season's), peeled and crushed
1 heaped tsp Dijon mustard
1 tbsp red wine vinegar
3 tbsp good-quality olive oil
sea salt and black pepper

Cook the red rice according to the packet instructions until *al dente*, about 35 minutes.

Meanwhile, throw the red onion, chilli, if using, radishes and tomatoes into a pretty serving bowl. Remove any tough outer leaves from the fennel, then cut into wafer-thin slices, using a mandolin, if you have one. Add to the bowl with the chopped herbs and spring onions. Crumble in the feta.

Toast the kalonji seeds, if using, in a hot, dry small frying pan for a minute and then toss them into the salad. Similarly, toast the pine nuts until they begin to turn oily and biscuity pale brown in colour; add these too.

For the dressing, combine the crushed garlic, mustard and wine vinegar in a large bowl, then whisk in the olive oil until the dressing emulsifies thickly. Season with salt and pepper to taste.

Drain the rice and tip it straight into the dressing. Toss to combine, then add to the salad bowl and gently toss everything together. Taste and adjust the seasoning, then serve.

FENNEL & CARAWAY SEED ROLLS

This is a start-the-night-before recipe, but that should not deter you – it will take you no longer to get the starter going than it takes to clean your teeth. Fresh yeast is always best, but nothing beats Rapunzel's organic fresh yeast. Go easy on the seeds, caraway can taste medicinal, but curiously, these rolls are as good with cheese or the smoked mackerel pâté on page 36 as they are with marmalade.

makes 12–15, depending on size

for the starter
130ml warm water (between hot and tepid)
a piece of fresh yeast, the size of a large walnut
150g stoneground wholewheat bread flour

for the dough
450g wholewheat bread flour
50g plain white flour
225g malted grain and brown bread flour (ideally Shipton Mill)
2 tsp sea salt
1 tbsp malt syrup (or molasses)
1 tbsp olive oil
2 level tsp caraway seeds
2 level tsp fennel seeds
about 300ml warm water (as above)
semolina, to sprinkle
beaten egg, to glaze
sesame and sunflower seeds, to finish

The night before, or at least 12 hours ahead, pour the 130ml warm water into a jug, crumble in the yeast and whisk until it dissolves. Put the 150g wholewheat flour into a large bowl and pour on the yeast liquid, allowing room for the mixture to treble in volume. Mix well and cover the bowl with cling film. Leave in a warm spot overnight.

The next morning, put the three flours, salt, malt syrup, olive oil and the caraway and fennel seeds into a large bowl and scrape the fermented starter on top. Add 280ml warm water and work with your hands until the dough comes together, adding more of the water as needed and making sure that the flour at the bottom of the bowl is all incorporated.

Turn the dough onto a floured surface. If it feels sticky-wet, simply shake extra white flour out onto the surface; if too dry, sprinkle with a little extra water. Work the dough with the heel of your hand so that it elongates like a baguette, then bring each end to the middle and repeat. Every so often, stretch the dough as far as it will go and roll it back towards you; this stretches the gluten. Keep it up for 5–10 minutes, then shape the dough into a ball and put back in the bowl. Cover with a slightly damp tea-towel and leave it to rise somewhere warm for an hour.

Preheat the oven to 220°C/Gas 7. Sprinkle some semolina evenly over a couple of baking trays. Turn the risen dough back onto a floured surface and knock it down, then cut into 12 or so equal pieces and shape into rolls. Place on the baking trays, spacing them apart. Cover with a large plastic bag, forming a tent that doesn't touch the dough, and leave in a warm place for the final 15 minute rise.

Uncover the rolls. Brush the surface with beaten egg and sprinkle some sesame and sunflower seeds on top. Bake for about 20 minutes, until the crust is golden and the rolls sound hollow when tapped on the base with your knuckles. Transfer to a wire rack to cool.

Wait until the rolls are just warm if you can restrain yourself – hot bread straight from the oven is delicious but indigestible!

AUBERGINE, RED ONION & ANCHOVY PISSALADIÈRE

Yeasted pastry, the sort that turns a tart into a galette, also works brilliantly for a pizza or pissaladière. Here the crust is so thin it crisps as delectably as toast. I could eat this dish weekly, just varying the topcoat with the seasons. When fresh artichokes are around, I strew a couple of quartered cooked hearts on with the cheese at the end. Stracchino, that lovely, lactic cow's cheese, oozes deliciousness, but mozzarella di bufala and burrata are good dolloped on top too.

serves 2–3 as a main dish; more as a canapé

for the dough

150g stoneground wholewheat bread flour (I use Shipton Mill), plus extra to sprinkle
1 tsp sea salt
a piece of fresh yeast, the size of a walnut
2 tbsp hand-hot water
1 egg
3 tbsp Jersey or other rich double cream
semolina, to sprinkle

for the topping

4-5 medium red onions
4 tbsp olive oil
a few thyme sprigs, leaves picked and chopped
sea salt and black pepper
1 aubergine (ideally the violet Sicilian variety)
a small tin of semi-cured anchovies, or anchovies in olive oil, drained
a handful of black olives, pitted (Ligurian or Taggiasca)
250g packet of stracchino, burrata or a mozzarella di bufala di campana

To make the dough, put the flour into a large bowl and sprinkle the salt around the edge. Crumble the yeast into a jug, add the water and whisk briskly to dissolve. Make a well in the flour, add the egg, yeast liquid and cream and mix to a wet dough. Sprinkle over a little more flour. Cover the bowl with a cloth and leave to rise in a warm place for about 2 hours or until the dough has doubled in volume.

Meanwhile, for the topping, peel, halve and finely slice the onions. Heat 2 tbsp olive oil in a heavy-bottomed frying pan over a very low heat and add the onions with the chopped thyme. Cook gently for about 30 minutes, sprinkling with a little salt at the start to draw out the moisture and covering the pan to stop the onions browning. Drain off their juice, then scrunch over some pepper.

While the onions are cooking, preheat the oven to 220°C/Gas 7. Cut the aubergine lengthways into slices, the thickness of a £1 coin. Brush a large baking tray with some of the remaining olive oil and lay the aubergine slices on it. Brush with the rest of the olive oil and roast for about 7 minutes or until soft when pierced with a skewer.

Scatter semolina evenly over another large baking tray and drop the ball of dough in the middle. Stretch the dough to the edges of the tin, pressing it out with floured fingers and sprinkling it with a little more flour if it becomes too sticky to work at any point. Make it as evenly thin as you can. Cover with cling film and leave to rise in a warm spot for 25 minutes.

Press the dough out again to the edges of the tin. Quickly spread the onion mixture evenly over the dough and top with the aubergine slices. Arrange lines of anchovies on top and scatter over the olives. Bake on the top shelf of the oven for 10–15 minutes until the edges are beginning to brown. Take out and quickly dollop on spoonfuls of stracchino, burrata or mozzarella. Immediately return to the oven for 2 minutes, no more.

Cut the pissaladière into slices or fingers and serve.

SPICED PARMESAN BISCUITS

Tapas time, happy hour, pre-prandials, what-you-will, a snifter is no good until you whet the taste buds too, and that absolutely has to be done with something salt. I've been making Parmesan biscuits for years now, often freezing or refrigerating the raw dough in cylinders until I'm ready to bake it. These biscuits are dusky, spicy and warming, a culture-mix of Italy and India. The main problem is stopping yourself from eating a rake of them, so exercise a little restraint with the quantity you cook, I guess. Or not.

makes about 24

1 heaped tsp each cumin, fennel, black mustard and kalonji (nigella) seeds
12 black peppercorns
2 small, mild red chillies
120g plain flour, sifted
120g chilled unsalted butter, cut into cubes
120g Parmesan, freshly grated

Heat a small frying pan over a medium heat, then throw in the cumin and fennel seeds. Toast for about a minute until they begin to brown and pop, then tip into a mortar and crush (a little finer than coarsely). Tip onto a plate and set aside.

Toast the mustard and kalonji seeds in the same way until they hop and pop in the pan, then add them whole to the crushed seeds on the plate. Coarsely crack the peppercorns using the pestle and mortar and add these too.

Grill the chillies or scorch by turning on a fork over a gas flame, until blistered on all sides, about 3 minutes. Put into a bowl, cover with cling film and leave until cool enough to handle. Peel away the skin, remove the seeds and slice the chillies into tiny strips. Set aside.

Put the flour, butter cubes and grated Parmesan into a food processor and process until the mixture has all but cohered. Add the spice mixture and pulse until the dough forms a ball.

Turn onto a lightly floured surface and work in the chillies with your fingers; don't worry about their moisture, just work it in. Shape the dough into a cylinder, wrap tightly in cling film and roll to neaten the shape. Refrigerate for at least a couple of hours or freeze until ready to use.

Preheat the oven to 200°C/Gas 6. Line a baking tray with non-stick baking paper and unwrap the cylinder of dough. Cut discs, the thickness of a £1 coin, and place on the lined tray, leaving space in between to allow for spreading. Bake on the middle oven shelf for 8–10 minutes until browned at the edges.

Leave on the baking tray for a couple of minutes to allow the biscuits to firm up, then transfer to a rack to cool a little. Eat warm.

BEGINNINGS

Beginnings are never sweet. It's a fact of life, a lore of the table. We crave sweet endings and salt, bitter beginnings. With, perhaps, a touch of piquancy. Whilst beginnings are designed to titillate the palate, whet the appetite for what's to come, the end should seduce and satisfy – sweetly, deftly, definitively.

In spring when the first asparagus spears shoot forth, we can dip them like green soldiers into runny hen's eggs. Or team them with little splotchy, inky shelled quail's eggs in a walnut oil dressed salad.

We can serve delicately bitter raw chicory, the maroon and white, with chunks of Alaskan wild salmon in a gently curried mayo. Or play a riff on mackerel pâté with hot-smoked mackerel, red onion, capers and horseradish. Or reinvent the trad chicken liver pâté smooth and elegantly spiced with a home-made quatre-épices of white peppercorns, ginger, cloves and nutmeg. Perhaps the simplest of showstoppers, a most dazzling Act I, is my pea and prosciutto mousse, ablaze with colour and sweet-salt flavour and as simple to make as you could wish for.

ASPARAGUS & QUAIL'S EGG SALAD

This is a dish of delicate simplicity. I have also made it with goose, duck and hen's eggs. A goose egg is a beauteous thing. It takes 7 minutes to cook after you've brought it to the boil. When halved, it spills its iron-rich crocus-coloured yolk – as sticky as glue and as renewing as spring, or life itself. Keeping the asparagus away from water preserves its verdant green. Like earth, air, fire and water, the four elements of this dish – egg, asparagus, lemon and emollient oil – are simplicity itself and all you need.

serves 2

12 homegrown asparagus spears, trimmed, woody ends snapped off
2 tbsp good, fruity olive oil
sea salt and black pepper
12 quail's eggs
grated zest of 1 lemon and a little spritz of juice
1–2 tbsp walnut oil, to taste

Cut the asparagus tips from the stalks and keep them separate. Now cut the stalks on the bias into shorter lengths (so that you have a larger cut surface area than you would from simply chopping into chunks). They cook more quickly like this and look prettier in the dish.

Heat the olive oil in a large, heavy-bottomed frying pan and throw in the asparagus stalks. Cook, turning, for a couple of minutes, then add the tips (which take less time to cook through) and sprinkle with a little salt. Once the tips have been added, the asparagus will take another 5 minutes or so to cook through, depending on thickness; test with a skewer.

While the asparagus is cooking, cook the quail's eggs: carefully add them to a small pan of boiling water, bring back to the boil and then simmer for 1½ minutes. Drain and briefly hold under cold running water until just cool enough to handle, then peel while still hot. (A bit of a fiddly task but worth it, and you can always seek help from your fellow diner.) Cut the eggs in half lengthways.

As soon as the asparagus is cooked, sprinkle with the lemon zest and remove the pan from the heat. Scrunch over some pepper, add a spritz of lemon juice to taste and trickle over the walnut oil. Taste and adjust the seasoning, adding a little more lemon juice or oil if needed. Tip the contents of the pan into a serving dish and add the halved quail's eggs. Serve warm with good home-made bread or my fennel and caraway seed rolls (on pages 26–7).

CHICORY WITH WILD SALMON & MANGO MAYONNAISE

The sleekly oily flesh of wild salmon has a flavour like no other and it is affordable if you buy Alaskan. Matched with a mango-ey curried mayo, left over from my Coronation crab (on pages 52–3), and the bitterness of the chicory to offset the sweet, this is a pre-dinner taste-bud sharpener of wondrous subtlety and surprise.

serves 8

750g piece filleted Alaskan wild salmon, about 750g and 2.5cm thick
sea salt and black pepper
1 tbsp olive oil
2–3 heaped tbsp curried mayonnaise (see page 52, or below)
2 Treviso (red chicory)
2 white chicory
1 tbsp chopped flat-leaf parsley

Cut the salmon into bite-sized cubes and season them lightly with salt and pepper. Heat the olive oil in a frying pan and cook the salmon cubes very briefly, turning until pink on all sides but with a thin seam of raw coloured salmon in the middle. Transfer to a bowl and set aside to cool.

Separate 4 outer chicory leaves from each head (save the smaller inner leaves for a salad); you will need 16 leaves in total. Arrange them, hollow side up, on a serving platter.

Divide the salmon between the chicory cavities and spoon a little curried mayo on top. Scatter with chopped parsley, grind over some pepper and serve.

NOTE

If you haven't any leftover home-made curried mayo to hand, flavour 2–3 heaped tbsp good-quality ready-made mayo with a little garam masala, a pinch of toasted ground cumin seeds and ½–1 tsp hot mango chutney to taste, adding a little yoghurt and/or double cream, too.

SMOKED MACKEREL PÂTÉ WITH CAPERS, RED ONION & ANCHOVY

Once upon a time – in the sixties – smoked mackerel pâté was a harsh, crude dish – like its stablemate staple, kipper pâté – easy to make but without the balance and subtlety that is necessary to offset good quality, oak-smoked fish. Try this version on some toasted rye bread and demur – in the tarry and linger sense of the word. Please adjust all the ingredients carefully. I find nearly three-quarters of a lemon's juice works with a wedge to serve, and restraint with the capers and red onion. The cracked black peppercorns are purely a matter of taste.

serves 6

180g packet good-quality hot smoked mackerel (ideally Summer Isles)
1½–2 tsp very, very finely chopped red onion
1½–2 tsp tiny capers, rinsed, drained and chopped
1–1½ tsp chopped dill, rinsed
2 heaped tbsp soured cream
juice of ½–1 lemon
1 heaped tsp hot horseradish (ideally The English Provender Co.)
60g unsalted butter, softened
2 good-quality anchovies (optional)
1 tsp cracked black peppercorns, or to taste

Put the mackerel fillets on a large plate and peel away the skin. Scatter over the red onion, chopped capers and dill. Spoon the soured cream on top and squeeze over the juice of ½ lemon. Add the hot horseradish. On the other side of the plate, mash the softened butter with the anchovies, if using.

Crack the peppercorns using a pestle and mortar and sift out the dusty remains, scooting the pepper bits onto the brew on the plate.

Mash everything on the plate together well, using a fork, until evenly amalgamated. Taste at this point and add more lemon juice and/or pepper if you think either is needed. Salt is unnecessary, as the mackerel, anchovy and capers provide sufficient.

When you are happy with the balance of flavours, fork the pâté into a little terrine, cover with a lid or cling film and refrigerate.

Serve chilled with toasted rye bread or with my fennel and caraway seed rolls (on pages 26–7), split and toasted.

CARPACCIO OF TUNA

You need thick fillets of yellowfin tuna for this glorious, yet simple starter. It takes a matter of minutes to assemble the dish, but you need to do so 3 or 4 hours ahead, to allow time for the subtle flavours to be drawn together in the fridge. Too much orange and lemon juice would 'cook' the fish like a ceviche. Let the oily fish speak for itself: foremost should be its taste and soft, almost meaty texture; in the background a touch of finely grated citrus and a slick of fruity olive oil ruffling the surface of the tender flesh.

serves 4

240–300g thick-cut tuna steaks, straight from the fridge
2 tsp salted baby capers, drained and dried
1 tsp finely grated orange zest, plus 1 tsp juice
1 tsp finely grated lemon zest, plus 1 tsp juice
1 tbsp fruity olive oil
sea salt and black pepper

Pare the tuna into fine slices, using a mandolin or a very sharp filleting knife, and lay them extravagantly on a large (preferably white) plate. Sprinkle over the baby capers and the grated orange and lemon zests. Sprinkle the citrus juices evenly over the surface and then trickle over the olive oil. Season with a little salt and pepper to taste.

Cover the plate with cling film and refrigerate for 2–3 hours. I like to remove the plate from the fridge about half an hour before eating, so that the carpaccio is cool rather than chilled or at room temperature. You really don't need bread or anything invasive to detract from the purity of taste and texture.

CHICKEN LIVER PÂTÉ WITH QUATRE-ÉPICES & THYME

My quest for the perfect chicken liver pâté is never ending. This is the smoothest, subtlest spiced and most velveteen to date. I make up a small batch of quatre-épices and keep it in a tiny jar for spicing up this pâté or anything with chicken livers, or porky dishes, like rillettes, which it suits equally well.

serves 4

360g organic/free-range chicken livers
a little milk, to soak
60g unsalted butter
1 small red onion, peeled
3 thyme sprigs, leaves only, chopped
sea salt and black pepper
1½ tbsp Cognac
1 tbsp Fino sherry
4 tbsp Jersey or other rich double cream
½–¾ tsp quatre-épices (see below)

to seal the pâté
60g unsalted butter

Trim the chicken livers, removing the membranes and tubes, then place in a bowl. Pour on enough milk to cover and leave to soak for an hour. Drain the chicken livers and pat dry.

Heat the butter in a frying pan over a gentle heat and coarsely grate about ½ tbsp red onion straight into the pan. Add the chopped thyme and some salt and pepper. Cook for a few minutes to soften. Add the whole chicken livers and cook on one side until browned, then the other; about 5 minutes in total. The livers should still be pink in the middle.

Pour in the Cognac and sherry and set alight. Once the flame has died down, pour in the cream and swirl around. The moment it begins to bubble, remove from the heat and pour into a blender. Add ½ tsp quatre-épices and blitz until smooth.

Push the chicken liver mixture through a sieve into a bowl, taste for seasoning and add extra quatre-épices and/or seasoning if needed. Scrape the pâté out into a small terrine or bowl and set aside to cool, then refrigerate.

Once the pâté is chilled, melt the butter for sealing gently and add a pinch of quatre-épices. Pour the butter over the surface of the pâté, keeping back the milky solids to discard. Return to the fridge.

Remove the pâté from the fridge 10 minutes before serving, with hot toast and perhaps some cornichons.

QUATRE-ÉPICES

Put 2 level tsp white peppercorns, ½ tsp ground ginger, 4 cloves and ⅓ tsp freshly grated nutmeg in a mortar and grind together with the pestle. Quatre-épices keeps well in a small corked or lidded spice jar, but the moment you feel the freshness and fragrance is somewhat diminished to the nose, discard and start again.

PEA & PROSCIUTTO MOUSSE WITH PARMESAN CREAM

This is one of those triumphal threesomes that is so delectable you wish you could manage a second one. The prosciutto is wound round the silken mousse like a scarf, and the burst of hot thick Parmesan cream is about as wicked as you could get. Beautiful, divine, and less damaging to your health than not eating it; after all, this is food to make you happy. Just don't think of serving a rich main course or a creamy pudding to follow.

serves 5

180g frozen peas
sea salt and black pepper
6 slices good-quality prosciutto (ideally sweet, nutty Gran Riserva)
2 large eggs
200ml Jersey or other rich double cream
freshly grated nutmeg

for the Parmesan cream
150ml Jersey or other rich double cream
2 heaped tbsp freshly grated Parmesan

Preheat the oven to 180°C/Gas 4. Lightly grease 5 dariole moulds. (If you don't have these, use ramekins, though rather than turrets you will end up with igloos, which won't look quite so bold and fortress-like on the plate, but will taste just as good.)

Add the peas to a pan of boiling salted water, bring back to the boil and cook for a few minutes until just tender. Drain and refresh under cold water; drain again, thoroughly.

Carefully lower a slice of prosciutto into each mould and gently spread it around with your fingers to line the mould. Use the sixth slice to patch and fill any gaps. The prosciutto should come to the top of the moulds and might overhang a little in places.

Tip the peas into a blender, add the eggs and blitz until smooth.

Scrape into a bowl and stir in the cream. Season with salt and pepper to taste and add a suspicion of nutmeg.

Divide the mixture between the prosciutto-lined moulds and gently flip any overhanging prosciutto on top. Cover with little hats of foil so that the mixture doesn't form a skin.

Stand the moulds in a high-sided roasting tin and pour in enough boiling water to come two-thirds of the way up the sides. Cook in the centre of the oven for 25–30 minutes until the mousses have just set, but still shudder softly in the middle when you shake them a little. If using ramekins, the mousses will take 5 minutes or so less to cook, so start checking these after 20 minutes.

Remove the moulds from their water bath and set aside while you make the Parmesan cream.

Pour the cream into a small pan and add the Parmesan. Bring slowly to the boil, whisking to melt and incorporate the cheese. After a couple of minutes, as the Parmesan melts, the sauce will thicken considerably. Season with a little pepper.

To unmould the mousses, run a knife around the inside of each mould and turn out onto warmed small plates. Pour a little of the Parmesan cream over each one and serve at once.

SOUP, BEAUTIFUL SOUP...

Beautiful soup, so rich and green,
Waiting in a hot tureen!
Who for such dainties would not stoop?
Soup of the evening, beautiful soup!

Soup can be dainty, refined, soup can be chunky, peasant, but the idea that a soup recipe is less of a proper recipe than a more solid bastion – a meaty, fishy, chunky thing you can really get your teeth into – is, I think, misplaced. Yes, soup is simple – more often than not. It rarely relies on strictness of measurement or ingredient: things can be more easily exchanged; differently herbed, spiced, finished; made poorer or richer, creamier or lighter, but that doesn't in itself mean a poverty of invention – quite the opposite.

I'm not so committed in the summer, though I do love the cold, oily-smooth richness of avocado and the feisty Spanish duo – gazpacho and ajo blanco; or a light, fruity cherry; or pale cucumber soup with a sharp hint of yoghurt and a smattering of cumin or dill.

The pot is really out in my kitchen by mid-October and I am beginning to think I can no longer pretend it's still summertime and summer food time. No, I won't turn the heating on yet, but I will have a hot pot of soup. It is often and always a treat.

Heading down into the dark days, think how the very word 'soup' soothes and cajoles us, as we envision the steaming pot and the nourishing-the-soul ingredients lying under its lid. We warm our cockles at the very notion of it.

Each leafy autumnal hue is reflected in our soup bowls, from the mealy yellow butternut to flame-orange squash; from the dank, below beech tree and hedge habitués, porcini, crimini, Portobello and chestnut mushrooms through taupe, dun, fawn, ivory; chestnut, haricot bean, hazelnut, parsnip, leek, not forgetting vibrant carrot and mossy green spinach.

In midwinter we turn soup stewy and stew soupy – with borlotti and cannellini beans, lentils and ham hocks, pasta, tomatoes, potatoes, Parmesan, croûtons, rice. We add bulk and bulwark and stand a spoon up in it, have a second bowl, call a stew a soup if the meat plays a mere bit part, probably just so that we can eat it with a spoon and get away with it.

Spoon feeding, that's the thing. It takes us back, it nourishes the soul. And nothing wrong with a bit of spoon feeding if that spoon is warm and gloriously full.

ROAST CHESTNUT & CARAMELISED GARLIC SOUP

November and the chestnuts are in from Italy and France, or you can pick them from the trees. Jars and vacuum packs are good enough for stuffing and puds, but soup needs the flavour and texture of the real thing. The richly velvet, mealy texture of this soup owes nothing to flour or cream or even chicken stock, and everything to the delicacy of the nut itself and the sweetness of the caramelised garlic.

serves 4, or 2 as a lunch or supper

350g chestnuts in shells
1 small head of garlic
2 tbsp olive oil
knob of butter (the size of a walnut)
1 shallot or small onion, peeled and finely sliced
sea salt and black pepper
1 bay leaf
generous 600ml water

Preheat the oven to 200–220°C/Gas 6–7. Score the chestnuts with a cross and roast them on a baking tray in the oven, or cook over an open fire, for around 12 minutes before testing with the tip of a knife. (Be careful – the chestnuts are liable to explode when they are ready – some of mine did!) Peel the chestnuts as soon as you can take the heat.

Meanwhile, put the head of garlic on the baking tray and trickle over half of the olive oil. Roast in the oven for about 20 minutes until soft when pierced with a knife tip. Pop the soft garlic cloves out of their skins onto a plate.

Heat the rest of the olive oil and the butter in a heavy-bottomed pan over a low heat. Add the shallot and sauté gently until beginning to soften, sprinkling a little salt over it. Throw in the peeled chestnuts and cook until they absorb the fat and oil, then add the garlic cloves, bay leaf and water. Bring to the boil, then lower the heat, cover and simmer gently for 15 minutes or until softened. Add a scrunch of pepper. Take out and reserve a few pieces of chestnut; remove and discard the bay leaf.

Purée the soup using a hand-held stick blender (or a free-standing one), then pass through a sieve into a clean pan. Reheat gently, then taste and adjust the seasoning with more salt if needed and a good scrunch of pepper. The soup will be thickly creamy and a sort of delicate roan, almost pink colour.

Scatter the remaining nubbles of chestnut in the bottom of each warm soup bowl before pouring in the soup.

RED ONION SQUASH, TOMATO & COCONUT SOUP

The dual elements here are fragrance and creaminess from the lemongrass and coconut respectively, but nothing pervades or oversteps its mark. There is acidity from the tomatoes and yoghurt, sweetness from the red onion and a fresh zing from kaffir lime leaves. It's a perfect autumnal soup in that it combines summer and winter ingredients and flavours and thus hits a note of leaf-fall and warm tones in one.

serves 4

½ red onion squash
2 tbsp olive oil
1 small onion (preferably red), peeled and finely chopped
½ each mild red and green chilli, chopped, with seeds
3 dried kaffir lime leaves
1 lemongrass stalk, outer woody leaves removed, finely chopped
2 tbsp chopped coriander
1 tbsp torn Thai basil, or ordinary basil, plus extra to serve
6 tomatoes, cut into chunks
900ml chicken stock or water
200ml tinned organic coconut milk
1 tbsp fish sauce (nam pla)
sea salt and black pepper
1 heaped tbsp sheep's milk yoghurt

Peel and deseed the squash, then cut into cubes and steam over boiling water in a steamer with a tight-fitting lid until *al dente*, 5–10 minutes. (Or sprinkle with a little olive oil, wrap in foil and roast at 190°C/Gas 5 until tender.)

Heat the olive oil in a heavy-bottomed saucepan. Add the chopped onion and chillies and cook until they begin to soften. Now add the squash cubes and stir to coat. Scrunch up the kaffir leaves and add them to the pan with the chopped lemongrass, most of the coriander (save a little for serving), and the torn basil. Cook gently, stirring occasionally, for 3–4 minutes, then add the tomatoes and cook over a medium heat for a further 3–4 minutes.

Ladle in the hot stock or water and add the coconut milk and nam pla. Add some seasoning and bring slowly to the boil, then simmer gently for a couple of minutes.

Purée the soup using a hand-held stick blender (or a free-standing one), then pass through a sieve into a clean pan. Taste and adjust the seasoning and heat to just below the boil. Add a ladleful to the yoghurt in a bowl, stir to amalgamate and then stir back into the soup off the heat.

Ladle the soup into warm bowls and sprinkle a little torn basil over each portion to serve.

THE BIG DISH

I want this bit of the book to really inspire you. I have cooked these dishes again and again and not just because it is my job to – I want all my friends and family to enjoy them too. And I know how easy it is to get stuck. The 'What shall I cook tonight?' refrain echoes down through the seasons when often all we need is an old dish tweaked, like my all-time Irish love – boiled bacon and cabbage, cooked here with pear perry and Cashel Blue.

If you don't like cooking new things for friends until you've had a dry run, you might change your mind with the utterly simple, wacky chicken breast pockets or the witty, hot summer skirt, depending, naturally, on the time of year, but skill-wise about as difficult as reading the recipe.

The fillet of venison – or lamb – with a spiced aubergine charlotte might sound palaverous. It isn't. It's roast tongues of aubergine furled over a soufflé dish with a spiced tomato sauce. The meat is browned and cooked in a frying pan. And if there's a veggie in the house, just don't give them the meat.

I can never resist a pie, and not just in the autumn or winter when the devastatingly delicious Roquefort and walnut pie is a must. In the early summer, when for a magical moment we have tiny broad beans, peas and asparagus, I make a primavera pie. Wrapped in a caul of prosciutto, dredged in creamy Parmesan and sealed in pastry, it makes me salivate just thinking about it. Look at the picture. You can do it. It is probably the best dish in this book. I will make it forever.

SALMON & SCALLOP CHOWDER

This is a lovely simple, yet sumptuous Saturday supper sort of a dish, or one for when you feel like luxury and comfort combined. Wild Alaskan salmon fillets are reasonably priced and give colour, texture and that wonderful oily richness that transports the dish to another level. I know classic chowders rely on smoked fish, but I've used some smoked rashers instead – not so many that either fish loses its oily or sweet-fleshed flavour. The potatoes must be cooked as gently as the fish so they don't break up.

serves 5

3 large potatoes, peeled and cut into large dice
60–75g unsalted butter
1 large red onion, peeled and finely chopped
2 celery stalks, de-strung with a potato peeler and chopped
120g or so crimini or chestnut mushrooms, wiped and halved
sea salt and black pepper
1 tbsp chopped tarragon
4 fillets Alaskan wild salmon, skinned
15–20 scallops, cleaned
3 rashers organic smoked back bacon, derinded
600ml milk
a bunch of spring onions (with green tops)

If the potatoes are of a starchy variety, rinse in a colander, then give them time to release some of their starch before washing again. Drain and pat dry. Melt the butter in a large, heavy-bottomed saucepan over a low heat and add the onion, celery, potatoes and mushrooms. Season with a little salt and pepper and add half the chopped tarragon. Cook gently, stirring carefully every so often, until all the vegetables have started to soften and turn translucent, about 10–15 minutes.

Meanwhile, cut the salmon into large bite-sized chunks. Separate the scallop corals, then halve each nugget of white scallop meat horizontally into two discs.

Cut the bacon rashers into thin strips and cook in a small frying pan, without additional fat, until crisp on both sides. Set aside.

Add the milk to the softened vegetables and bring slowly to scalding point, then put the lid on and allow to cook gently at a bare simmer. After 15 minutes, spike a potato cube gently right through with a skewer to see if it is cooked; it should be just a tiny bit resistant, no more. If so, remove the pan from the heat, plop in the salmon chunks and put the lid back on. The salmon will cook through gently in the residual heat of the milk.

When you are ready to serve, cut the white spring onions from their green tops and chop both, keeping them separate. Gently reheat the chowder and add the scallop discs and white spring onion as the milk begins to warm. When the milk is almost at a simmer, add the scallop corals and turn down the heat. As soon as the white scallop discs have turned opaque, after about a minute, remove the pan from the heat. Taste and adjust the seasoning, then scatter over the green spring onion, bacon and the rest of the tarragon.

Ladle the chowder into warm, large soup bowls and serve, with a salad to follow: a chicory and radicchio or Treviso salad in a mustardy dressing would be perfect.

GRILLED MACKEREL WITH PICKLED CUCUMBER

I have always been drawn to the indigenous ingredients of wherever I am, and by that, I don't mean just the rare and expensive ones like wild salmon, and truffles from Alba. To me, bounty and beauty in nature, in natural ingredients, are one and the same.

I'm not at all sure that if there were only one fish left in the sea and I had to choose it, it wouldn't be a mackerel. Close call with a spiny lobster, but there it is. I love the bold, firm, petrol-coloured fish with its black-backed hieroglyphs, its succulent oily flesh and its intense flavour.

The oiliness needs a little sharp pickle and a tang of citrus to set it off, and the melting tenderness of my newly invented Tamasin's potatoes. Crisp and browned beneath and meltingly fondant-middled, I slice them, reeking of garlic, like a cake straight out of the frying pan.

serves 4

4 very fresh mackerel, gutted and cleaned (heads intact)
sea salt and black pepper

for the pickled cucumber
1 large cucumber
2 tbsp tarragon vinegar or white wine vinegar
1–2 tsp unrefined granulated sugar
2 tsp finely chopped tarragon leaves
grated zest of 1 lime
1–2 tsp lime juice

First prepare the pickled cucumber. Peel the cucumber, cut it in half lengthways and scoop out the seeds with a teaspoon. Slice very thinly and leave in a colander to drain.

Meanwhile, mix the vinegar with 1 tsp sugar in a bowl, stirring until dissolved, then add the chopped tarragon, some seasoning, the lime zest and 1 tsp lime juice. Taste and adjust accordingly, adding more sugar, lime juice and/or seasoning as needed, balancing sweetness with acidity.

Tip the cucumber into a serving bowl and pour over the pickle liquor. Toss to mix, then taste and adjust again if necessary.

Preheat the grill to its highest setting. Line the grill pan with foil. Season the mackerel with salt and pepper and lay on the grill rack. Grill the fish for 6–8 minutes, depending on their size, then turn and cook for a further 5 minutes or until a knife inserted in the thickest part of the flesh slides through easily, and the skin is bubbling, crisp and beginning to blacken.

Place a grilled mackerel on each warm serving plate and spoon over the oily juices from the grill pan. Add a portion of the potatoes and a heaped spoonful of the cucumber pickle.

TAMASIN'S POTATOES

Peel about 650g potatoes and slice finely, ideally using a mandolin or the fine slicing disc on a food processor. Immerse in a bowl of cold water for 20 minutes to remove excess starch. Generously butter a heavy-bottomed (ideally cast-iron) frying pan. Drain the potatoes and pat dry in a tea-towel. Spread 2 tbsp olive oil over the base of the frying pan and add a knob of butter. Layer a third of the potato slices in the pan, scatter over a couple of finely chopped anchovies and ½–1 sliced garlic clove, then season and dot with butter and oil. Repeat these layers twice.

Put the pan over a gentle heat and when the potatoes begin to fry, turn the heat up to medium for a few minutes. Cover with a lid, reduce the heat again and cook for about 30 minutes, checking at intervals that the potatoes on the bottom are not burning.

Uncover and lift the bottom layer of potatoes carefully with a palette knife; it should be somewhere between golden and brown. Push a skewer down through the middle to test whether the potatoes are cooked or nearly cooked. Accordingly, turn up the heat and cook a little longer until the bottom is dark brown and crisp, in contrast to the melting-textured top. In total, the potatoes take 40–50 minutes. Let rest for a couple of minutes before cutting into wedges to serve.

CORONATION CRAB WITH SPICED RED RICE & SAUTÉED ASPARAGUS

This is an early summer dish for when the crabs are sweet and meaty, asparagus is still being cut, and cold food begins to take your fancy. You either love or abjure coronation chicken. I love it and thought I'd try a crabby version, flavouring the mayo with garam masala, lime, chilli and mango chutney, with a surrounding coronet of red rice and spiced onion, toasted almonds, raisins, chopped coriander and sprigs of bunched watercress. You can prepare the whole dish in advance, so it is brilliant, temperamentally, if you don't want to be tied to time.

serves 4

1 large dressed crab, about 400–450g
1 large bunch of watercress, well washed
1 tsp kalonji (nigella) seeds, toasted

for the curried mayonnaise
1 large egg yolk
1 heaped tsp Dijon mustard
up to 300ml good-quality oil (I use half olive, half groundnut)
juice of 1 lime
juice of ½ lemon
up to 2 heaped tsp garam masala
a knife tip of cayenne pepper, to taste
1 tsp cumin seeds, toasted and ground
1–2 heaped tbsp hot mango chutney
1 tbsp double cream, or more
1 heaped tbsp yoghurt
sea salt and black pepper

for the rice
300g red Camargue (or other nutty) rice
2 tbsp olive oil
1 large onion, peeled and sliced
⅓ tsp cayenne pepper
1 tsp cumin seeds, toasted and crushed
1 heaped tbsp raisins, soaked in hot water for 20 minutes and drained
2 tbsp chopped coriander
2 tbsp flaked almonds, lightly toasted

Pick over the white and dark crabmeat, checking for any fragments of shell, then tip into a bowl.

For the mayonnaise, mix the egg yolk and mustard together in a bowl. Gradually whisk in the oils, drop by drop to begin with until the mayo begins to thicken, and then in a steady stream. Once the mayo is thick, incorporate the lime juice and then a little of the lemon juice. Now stir in the spices and chutney, followed by the cream and yoghurt. Season with salt and pepper to taste. You may wish to add a little more lemon juice and/or cream for a more sauce-like consistency.

Stir 2 heaped tbsp of the mayo into the crabmeat, then taste and add a little more if you think it needs it. The mayo should bring out the flavour of the crab, not overwhelm it. Let stand at room temperature for an hour or two before serving to allow the flavours to mingle.

Meanwhile, cook the rice according to the packet instructions until *al dente*. Heat the olive oil in a frying pan over a medium-high heat and sauté the onion until browned, adding the spices and some salt after a few seconds. Take off the heat. The moment you drain the rice, stir in the spiced onion, raisins and chopped coriander.

Spoon the rice in a ring onto a large plate and scatter the almonds on top. Pile the crab in the middle and sprinkle over the kalonji seeds. Surround with a garland of watercress. Serve with sautéed asparagus.

A dish fit for king, queen, coronet, baronet, coronation.

NOTE

You'll have more curried mayo than you need for this recipe. Keep the rest in a jar in the fridge and use within a couple of weeks. (It is also used in the starter on page 35.) If you're not a mayonnaise maker, buy a really good tub to flavour, and taste all the way, balancing the acidity, heat and oiliness, as well as the sweetness from the chutney.

SAUTÉED ASPARAGUS

Allow 6 asparagus spears per person. Trim off the woody ends, then slice the spears on the diagonal. Heat 2 tbsp good, fruity olive oil in a large heavy-bottomed frying pan, add the asparagus with a little salt and sauté for 8–10 minutes until tender when tested with a knife, but still verdant green. Remove from the heat and add a good scrunch of pepper and the grated zest of 1 large lemon. Let cool to warm, then toss and serve.

DEBORAH'S SEAFOOD & NOODLE SALAD

My cousin Deborah has contributed a recipe to each of my cookery books, and one of the things I like about her food is that it isn't like mine. Our mutual love of food goes back to shared family lunches at our grandparents' table, with the scent of oak fires and roasting beef the moment you entered the door. Irreplaceable, the earliest memories of food are as irresistible as the dishes we recall from our past. How changed our cooking is now, but the constant is the love of food itself, the shared passion and its unashamed place in our lives.

serves 4

300g fresh Chinese noodles
4 slices smoked salmon (ideally wild Alaskan), cut into strips
200g shelled cooked prawns
2 spring onions, trimmed and finely shredded
small bunch of coriander, chopped
1 iceberg lettuce, outer leaves only

for the dressing
1 red chilli, deseeded and finely chopped
a small finger of fresh root ginger, finely grated
5 tbsp mild-flavoured oil (such as sunflower)
1 tbsp sesame oil
finely grated zest and juice of 1 lime
a few drops of Tabasco
2 tbsp tamari or shoyu sauce
1 tsp Thai fish sauce
black pepper

First make the dressing. Combine the chilli and grated ginger in a bowl and whisk in all the other ingredients, seasoning with a little pepper. Taste and adjust the flavours as necessary.

Cook the noodles according to the instructions on the packet, drain and toss them in the dressing while still hot.

Allow the dressed noodles to cool until barely warm, then stir in the smoked salmon strips, prawns, shredded spring onions and chopped coriander.

Arrange a nest of lettuce leaves on each plate and pile a portion of the seafood and noodle salad in the middle to serve.

WILD SALMON WITH POTATOES & GRIDDLED TREVISO

If you, like me, will only eat salmon that has had a life (rather than the farmed stuff), Alaskan wild salmon is reasonably priced and one way of getting to eat this magnificent fish. It is on the market in the autumn and winter – when red chicory is available and I want a dish of warm tones and palette. I use Roseval potatoes, which have a deep pink skin and are waxy, like a salad potato. I am not generally keen on shelf-stacking a plate and cheffy twizzles, but in this case, three elements – fish, veg and potato – are piled one on t'other and anointed with the sauce.

serves 2

6–8 medium Roseval (or Pink Fir Apple or Anya) potatoes
1 tbsp olive oil, plus a little extra for brushing
4 Treviso (red chicory) or white chicory, halved lengthways
½ lemon
2 Alaskan wild salmon fillets, about 180g each

for the sauce
1 lemongrass stalk, outer woody leaves removed, finely chopped
1 tsp grated fresh horseradish or ⅓–½ tsp hot horseradish (English Provender, not the creamed variety)
1 tsp finely grated fresh root ginger
1 tbsp crème fraîche
1 tsp olive oil
2 tsp freshly squeezed orange juice
sea salt and black pepper

First make the sauce. Using a pestle and mortar, crush the chopped lemongrass, then mix in the horseradish and ginger. Stir in the crème fraîche, followed by the olive oil and orange juice, then season with salt and pepper. Taste and adjust the flavours if you need to – don't allow the horseradish to predominate. Set aside.

Boil the potatoes until just tender. Meanwhile, brush a griddle or a heavy-bottomed frying pan with olive oil and place over a medium heat. Add the chicory halves, cut side down, and sprinkle over a little salt. Cook for 3–4 minutes, then turn, using tongs, and cook for a further 3 minutes or until the core yields to a knife point. Remove the pan from the heat and squeeze a little lemon juice over the chicory.

While the chicory and potatoes are cooking, heat a small frying pan over a medium heat and add 1 tbsp olive oil. Check the salmon for any pin-bones, then lay the salmon fillets in the pan, skin side down, season and cook until you can see the flesh has turned pale pink almost halfway through the thickness. Turn over and repeat but leave a narrow stripe of raw-looking salmon in the middle (to avoid overcooking). Remove from the heat.

As soon as the potatoes are cooked, drain and slice them lengthways while still hot.

Divide half of the sliced potatoes between two warm serving plates and spoon over a little dollop of the sauce. Place two griddled chicory halves on each pile and then spoon the rest of the potato slices on top and add a little more sauce. Add the last chicory halves and top with the cooked salmon fillets. Drop a final blob of sauce on the fish and serve warm, rather than piping hot.

CREAMY SALMON & LEEK TART WITH ROSEMARY

This mosaic of pink and green is a beauty to behold and balanced, ingredient by ingredient, so no one thing stands out or passes by unnoticed. Salmon is easily overwhelmed in a crowd. Here it is cubed and introduced raw into the pastry, so it doesn't over-cook. I wanted something deep – a full-bodied, deep-bellied tart, with sweet, buttery leeks offset by lactic crème fraîche and astringent rosemary.

serves 4

for the pastry
120g plain flour
pinch of sea salt
60g chilled unsalted butter, cut into cubes
1–1½ tbsp ice-cold water
a little egg white, for brushing

for the filling
4 fat leeks, well washed
30g butter
½ tbsp or so olive oil
2 tsp finely chopped rosemary needles
sea salt and black pepper
4 salmon fillets (ideally wild Alaskan), about 180g each
250ml carton crème fraîche
2 large eggs, plus 2 extra yolks

To make the pastry, sift the flour and salt into a food processor, add the butter cubes and pulse briefly until the mixture resembles crumbs. Add 1 tbsp water through the feeder tube and process just until the dough comes together in a ball, adding more of the water if necessary. Wrap in cling film, flatten slightly with the palm of your hand and chill in the fridge for 30 minutes.

Meanwhile, grease a 23cm cake tin or deep flan tin. Trim the coarse tops from the leeks, retaining most of the green part, then chop the leeks. Melt the butter with the olive oil in a heavy-bottomed frying pan over a low heat, then add the rosemary needles and cook for about 30 seconds until sizzling. Now add the leeks with a little salt, stir for a few minutes, then cover with a lid. Sweat gently for about 15 minutes until almost tender and wilted. Scrunch over some pepper, then tip into a sieve over a bowl and leave to drain.

Preheat the oven to 180°C/Gas 4 and place a baking sheet inside to heat up. Skin the salmon and cut into large chunks, checking for any pin-bones. In a bowl, whisk together the crème fraîche, eggs, egg yolks and some seasoning until evenly combined. Add the buttery leek juices too.

Roll out the pastry on a lightly floured surface and use to line the prepared tin, leaving the excess overhanging the rim of the tin. Line the pastry case with a sheet of greaseproof paper or non-stick baking paper and a layer of baking beans. Bake 'blind' on the hot baking sheet in the oven for 20 minutes. Remove the paper and beans. Prick the base and sides of the pastry case with a fork, brush with a little egg white and bake for a further 5 minutes.

Lay the chunks of salmon in the pastry case and intersperse with the leeks. Pour over the creamy egg mixture and return to the oven. Bake for 30–40 minutes until the top is browned and the filling is set. Transfer to a wire rack and leave to stand for 10 minutes before serving. A lightly dressed green salad that includes some peppery leaves and a few finely chopped spring onions is all you'll need on the side.

BAKED SARDINES WITH ORANGE GREMOLATA

A dish to serve cooler than hot in the summer, once you have let the gremolata flavours permeate the fish. I think orange, rather than the classic lemon zest in a gremolata, works beautifully with any oily fish.

If you are lucky, your fishmonger will scuff the scales off the sardines for you; if you are not, it doesn't take too long. And in the absence of spankingly fresh sardines, I am always happy with a box of frozen Portuguese sardines, which are frozen as soon as they are caught and are the next best thing.

serves 4–8

24 sardines, descaled (3 or 4 each for a starter, 6 for a main course)
a little olive oil
sea salt and black pepper

for the gremolata
grated zest of 1 orange
2 tbsp finely chopped parsley
1 large garlic clove, peeled and crushed

Preheat the oven to 200°C/Gas 6. Lay the sardines in a single layer on a lightly oiled baking tray and trickle a little more olive oil over them. Season with pepper and a little salt. Bake in the oven for 6–7 minutes or until a skewer inserted in the thickest part of the flesh passes softly right through.

Meanwhile, mix the gremolata ingredients together on a plate. Transfer the baked sardines to individual plates or a warm large platter and sprinkle with the gremolata. Let stand for 5 minutes or so, then serve. Simplicity itself.

POTATO GNOCCHI WITH ASPARAGUS, OLIVES & TOMATOES

When a New Zealand chef friend, Peter Gawron, turned up unexpectedly for a flying visit in the early summer, the first thing we did was talk food and hit the stove together. We cooked this stunning early-summer supper, each contributing ideas, ingredients and timings to the equation. (*Illustrated on previous page*)

serves 6

for the gnocchi
250g red onion squash (for colour), or use butternut
600g floury potatoes, such as King Edward, peeled
sea salt
about 180g plain flour
2–3 tbsp semolina

Preheat the oven to 200°C/Gas 6. Cut the squash into crescent slices, scooping out the seeds with a spoon, then place on a lightly oiled baking tray. Roast for 30 minutes or until tender. Meanwhile, boil the potatoes in salted water in the usual way until tender.

Scoop the cooked squash pulp from the rind and drain the potatoes well. Push the hot squash and potato flesh through the coarse disc of a mouli (food mill) or a potato ricer straight onto a floured surface (or mash together thoroughly in a bowl, then turn out). Immediately add most (but not all) of the flour and mix with your hands until you have a smooth, slightly sticky dough. If it seems too wet, incorporate more of the flour.

Bring a large, heavy-bottomed pan of salted water to the boil. Meanwhile, with floured hands, roll the dough into a long cylinder, about 2.5cm in diameter. Cut into 2cm lengths and shape into little torpedo-like ovals. Dunk them in a little more flour to coat all over, shaking off the excess, and plop them onto a large plate scattered with semolina. Put a well-buttered large gratin dish in the oven to warm.

for the sauce
a bundle of asparagus, cleaned and trimmed, woody ends snapped off
2 tbsp olive oil
1 new season's garlic clove, peeled and sliced
12 Mammuth or 24 smaller green olives, pitted and sliced
about 24 ripe datari or cherry tomatoes, halved
finely grated zest of 1 lemon, plus a squeeze of juice
2 tbsp mascarpone
sea salt and black pepper
knob of butter (the size of a walnut)
60g Parmesan, freshly grated
60g pecorino, freshly grated
a few sprigs of savory, parsley or basil, chopped

For the sauce, cut the asparagus spears into short lengths. Warm the olive oil gently with the sliced garlic in a large, heavy-bottomed frying pan, then add the chopped asparagus. Cook gently, shaking the pan and turning the spears gently every so often, until *al dente*; they will take 7–8 minutes to reach this stage.

In the meantime, cook the gnocchi in a couple of batches: drop half of them into the boiling water with a spoon, spacing them apart, and keep the water at a gentle simmer. When the gnocchi start rising to the surface, allow them another 3 minutes, then scoop them out with a slotted spoon and plop them into the gratin dish with a little of their water to keep them moist. Pop them into the oven to keep warm while you cook the second lot.

Throw the sliced olives in with the asparagus and toss to heat through, then add the tomatoes and warm through only (so they hold their shape). Quickly add the lemon zest and mascarpone and stir in briefly. Season well and add a knob of butter and a spritz of lemon juice before tasting, adjusting and removing from the heat.

Tip the sauce onto the cooked gnocchi and scatter over some of the duo of grated cheeses; serve the rest in a bowl on the side for people to help themselves. I sprinkle chopped savory over the dish before serving, but if you don't have any, a little parsley or basil is fine.

PASTA WITH AUBERGINE, SQUASH, SPINACH & TOASTED PUMPKIN SEEDS

The fact that you can do the main stuff of this dish and then leave it assembled ready to gratinée makes it eminently suitable for unreliable arrivers or when simply wanting another drink before dinner. Caramelising the garlic and pounding it to a cream really gives this dish its identity, as does scoring and oiling the aubergines so that they are tender and creamy when cooked. Great for vegetarians.

serves 6

1 medium butternut squash
sea salt and black pepper
olive oil
2 aubergines
1 large head of garlic
500g penne or rigatoni
450g spinach, well washed
40–50g butter
2–3 heaped tbsp crème fraîche
1 tbsp pumpkin seeds
90g Parmesan (or half Parmesan, half pecorino), freshly grated

Preheat the oven to 200°C/Gas 6. Cut the squash into large chunks, removing the seeds. Place in one side of an oiled, large roasting tin and add a scrunch of salt and a sprinkle of olive oil.

Halve the aubergines lengthways and score the flesh deeply, without cutting right through the skin. Place in the roasting tin alongside the squash and trickle olive oil over the scored flesh, allowing it to run into the cuts. Season. Place the head of garlic in the tin too and sprinkle over 1 tsp olive oil.

Bake for 25–30 minutes until the vegetables feel tender when tested with a skewer and the garlic is soft. Pop the garlic cloves out of their papery cases and crush them with a little salt, using a pestle and mortar. Remove the skin from the squash, then cut into cubes. Scrape the aubergine pulp from the skins, cut into cubes and set aside on a plate with the squash.

Bring a large saucepan of salted water to the boil, shoot in the pasta and stir until it comes back to the boil. Be guided by the cooking time suggested on the packet, but drain when the pasta is slightly on the firm side of *al dente* (as it is going to be baked in the oven), retaining a little of the cooking water with the pasta as you tip it back into the pan.

Meanwhile, briefly cook the spinach in a large pan with just the water clinging to the leaves after washing, over a lively heat, until barely wilted. Drain in a colander, pressing out the water. Return to the pan, add 40g butter and heat briefly until melted. Remove from the heat and stir in 2 heaped tbsp crème fraîche and the garlic pulp.

Heat a dry small frying pan, throw in the pumpkin seeds and toast, pushing them around in the pan, for a couple of minutes until lightly coloured. Tip out onto a plate.

Add the garlicky spinach to the pasta and stir to combine. If the pasta looks a little dry still, stir in another generous tbsp crème fraîche and another knob of butter. Add the cubed squash and aubergines and toss together, seasoning well. Tip into a gratin dish, trickle over some olive oil to lubricate, then scatter over the toasted pumpkin seeds and grated Parmesan. (You can prepare ahead to this stage.)

When ready, place in the oven and bake for 25 minutes or until golden and bubbling. You may like to pass round a bowl of extra grated Parmesan for guests to help themselves.

ROQUEFORT & WALNUT PIE WITH A PEPPER & PARMESAN CRUST

I am writing this fresh from eating it. The full two irresistible slices. A great marriage under a punchy, peppery crust; the goo and salt of the blue, the crunch of the nut, the starch of the spud, the cohesion brought about with sweet onion, oregano and cream. The pastry was a last-minute inspiration, as flavoured pastries are not always to my taste, but a leftover spoonful of Parmesan and a teaspoon of cracked black peppercorns gave character and feist. The pastry quantity might not seem enough to you for a double-decker, but I can assure you it is. It's a slim, elegant, crisp crust, not a wodge of stodge.

serves 6–8

for the pastry

180g plain flour
90g chilled unsalted butter, cut into cubes
1 heaped tbsp freshly grated Parmesan
1–2 tbsp ice-cold water
1 heaped tsp black peppercorns, cracked in a mortar but not too finely, the dusty bits then sifted out
1 egg yolk, beaten with 1 tsp water, to glaze

for the filling

30g unsalted butter
1 large red onion, peeled and finely sliced
1 celery stalk (with leaves), de-strung with a potato peeler and chopped
3 oregano sprigs, chopped
45g Serre or other good walnuts, broken in half
4 tbsp double cream
2 large eggs
150g Roquefort

To make the pastry, sift the flour into a food processor and add the butter and Parmesan. Pulse until the mixture resembles crumbs, then add 1 tbsp cold water and pulse until it coheres into a ball, adding a bit more water if necessary. Stop immediately and take out the dough.

On a lightly floured surface, flatten the ball with the palm of your hand and scatter over the cracked peppercorns. Roll briefly and lightly to distribute the pepper, but do not overwork. Wrap the dough in cling film and leave to rest in the fridge for 30 minutes while you make the filling.

For the filling, melt the butter in a heavy-bottomed pan, add the onion and celery (with leaves) and cook gently until softened, about 15 minutes. Stir in the oregano and walnuts, then allow to cool slightly.

In a large bowl, lightly whisk the cream and eggs together to combine, then crumble in the Roquefort. While the onion mixture is still warm, tip it into the egg and cream mixture and gently fold it all together. You do not need any additional seasoning; the blue cheese is salty and the pepper is in the crust.

Preheat the oven to 190°C/Gas 5 and put a baking tray inside to heat up. Lightly grease a shallow 23cm tart dish. Divide the pastry in two, making one piece smaller (for the lid). Roll out the larger piece and use to line the tart dish, leaving the excess pastry overhanging the edge. Roll out the other piece for the lid.

Spoon the filling into the pastry case, brush the pastry edge with water and place the pie lid on top. Crimp the pastry edges together with the tines of a fork and brush the top with the beaten egg yolk. Bake for 30 minutes, then check the pie. It will probably need a further 10 minutes in the oven to bronze the pastry.

Leave the pie to stand on a wire rack for 10 minutes before cutting and serving with a green salad. It's also good eaten at room temperature – as a more-ish supper, or picnic or lunch-box treat.

PORCINI, CHESTNUT MUSHROOM & PROSCIUTTO LASAGNA

This is a seriously special dish. Up there with the best in the book, and it doesn't take nearly so long to make as a classic *lasagna*. I soak the dried porcini for far longer than the packet says (at least 8 hours) to get the salty, shardy 'shrooms really soft and fleshy tender.

There is always debate on whether one should, or should not, cook a cornucopia of funghi together, especially when you have the king of the forest, porcini, and might not want to interrupt or lessen the impact of their unique flavour. My feeling is that once dried, porcini are so much more intensely flavoured than when fresh, they can hold their own magisterially. Oyster, crimini and/or chestnut mushrooms will complement and add to the flavour and texture of the dish; a tiny amount of dried porcini goes an awful long way. The prosciutto is a lovely balancing act, and the caramelised garlic adds sweetness and depth.

serves 6

25g packet of dried porcini, soaked overnight in warm water
300g each chestnut, crimini and oyster mushrooms (or any combination of these)
1 head of garlic
2 tbsp good-quality olive oil
sea salt and black pepper
120g butter
3–4 tbsp Marsala
freshly grated nutmeg
900ml whole milk (or half milk, half hot chicken or game stock)
1 bay leaf
2 tbsp plain flour
4 tbsp single cream
10–12 very thin slices of prosciutto, rolled and cut into julienne strips
small bunch of basil, leaves stripped and torn
1 packet of good-quality dried lasagna (preferably no-need-to-precook)
90g each Parmesan and pecorino, freshly grated

Preheat the oven to 200°C/Gas 6. Drain the porcini in a sieve over a bowl, keeping the soaking water but making sure that any grit is discarded. Wipe the fresh mushrooms carefully with a damp cloth to remove all dirt, then slice thinly.

Put the garlic on a small roasting tray, douse with 1 tbsp olive oil and bake in the oven for about 25 minutes until soft when pierced with a knife tip. Pop the garlic cloves out of their papery skins and, when cool enough to handle, squish the garlic on a plate with a little salt to a paste, using a fork.

Heat 25g of the butter in a small frying pan, add the sliced porcini and fry gently for a minute or so. Add 1 tbsp Marsala and cook for about 10 minutes until soft.

At the same time, heat 35g butter in a large frying pan and add the sliced fresh mushrooms. Fry them gently, seasoning with a little salt, until their juices begin to exude. At this point, turn the heat up, splash a glug of Marsala into the pan and let it bubble and reduce right down, then repeat. Lower the heat and continue to cook until the mushrooms are softened and sticky with juice, then take the pan off the heat.

Add a scrunch of black pepper to both pans and some grated nutmeg to the fresh mushrooms.

To make the béchamel, heat the milk in a pan with the bay leaf. Melt the remaining 60g butter in another saucepan, stir in the flour and cook for a minute or until you have a pale biscuit coloured roux.

Now whisk in the hot milk (or milk and hot stock), a ladleful at a time. Add the liquor from the soaked porcini and simmer gently for 15 minutes, stirring from time to time. Stir in the cream, then taste and adjust the seasoning.

To assemble, spread a little béchamel over the base of a large baking dish. Pour a third of the remaining sauce into the porcini pan and the rest into the mushroom pan. Add the garlic paste to the mushroom pan with some of the prosciutto. Add the torn basil and the rest of the prosciutto to the porcini pan.

Put the first layer of lasagna on top of the béchamel in the gratin dish. Spoon over a third of the fresh mushroom mixture, sprinkle over a layer of mixed Parmesan and pecorino and cover with another layer of lasagna. Repeat these layers. Now spoon over all the porcini mixture and scatter with grated cheese. Add another layer of lasagna, then the rest of the fresh mushrooms and finish with a generous layer of cheese. (You can prepare ahead to this stage and refrigerate overnight, bringing the dish back to room temperature before baking.)

When ready, place the lasagna dish in the oven and bake for 30–40 minutes until golden and bubbling and the lasagna feels cooked right through when pierced with a skewer. Wait for 5 minutes before you serve it. A simple green salad afterwards is all you need.

VARIATION

For a vegetarian version, replace the prosciutto with 450g or so of rainbow or ordinary chard. Separate the stalks from the leaves and steam the stalks for 3–4 minutes until just tender, adding the torn leaves after a couple of minutes. Drain well and chop together in the colander. Alternate layers of chard with the funghi, covering the chard with béchamel. The curious, sweet earthiness of the chard is a delicate and surprising foil for the mushrooms.

PRIMAVERA & PROSCIUTTO PIE

The conflation of all things green and tiny in the Garden of Eden happens in June. There is still asparagus, there are baby artichokes, which you could add a few heads of, and the first of the broad beans and peas. And the mint is rising with the sap, searching tendrils of root spreading, if you'll let them, ready for the last of the Jersey Royals and the first of the peas.

What better than to try to contain all this bounty together, wrapped in a caul of prosciutto, with a gentle trickle of Jersey cream, egg yolks and Parmesan to bind. Have pie, will travel. Make this a deep-dish pie in a cake tin and you can transport it on a picnic and reveal its pink and green depths still warm when you arrive, even if it's only into your own back garden.

serves 4

for the shortcrust pastry

350g plain flour
pinch of sea salt
175g chilled unsalted butter, cut into cubes
1½ –2 tbsp ice-cold water
1 egg yolk, beaten with 1 tsp milk, to glaze

for the filling

12 asparagus spears, trimmed of woody ends
2 tbsp olive oil
sea salt and black pepper
180g freshly podded broad beans
180g freshly podded peas
6 slices prosciutto
2 tsp chopped mint
2 tsp chopped tarragon
4 cooked baby artichoke hearts, quartered (optional)
2 egg yolks
4 tbsp Jersey or other rich double cream
3–4 tbsp freshly grated Parmesan

To make the pastry, sift the flour and salt into a food processor, add the butter cubes and pulse briefly until the mixture resembles crumbs. Add 1½ tbsp water through the feeder tube and process just until the dough comes together in a ball, adding more of the water if necessary.

Divide the dough into two pieces, one slightly larger than the other. Wrap each in cling film, flatten slightly with the palm of your hand and chill in the fridge for 30 minutes. Meanwhile, grease a deep 20cm cake tin.

For the filling, slice the asparagus spears across into strips. Heat the olive oil in a frying pan, add the asparagus with a little salt and sauté for about 8–10 minutes until tender. Remove from the heat, season with pepper to taste and set aside to cool.

Blanch the broad beans in boiling salted water for 2 minutes, drain and refresh in cold water, then slip the beans out of their skins and add to the asparagus. Blanch the peas in simmering water for 3–4 minutes until tender. Drain and add to the vegetables in the frying pan.

Preheat the oven to 180°C/Gas 4 with a baking sheet inside to heat up. Roll out the larger piece of pastry on a lightly floured surface and use to line the prepared cake tin, leaving the excess overhanging the rim of the tin. Lay 4 prosciutto slices in the pastry case, to come a little way up the side. Add the chopped herbs and artichoke hearts, if using, to the cooled vegetables, toss through and then pile into the prosciutto-lined pastry case. Beat the egg yolks and cream together and pour over the vegetables, then sprinkle with the Parmesan.

Roll out the other piece of pastry for the lid and lay it over the top of the pie. Press the pastry edges together and trim away the excess pastry. Seal the edges with the tines of a fork and brush the pastry lid with the egg glaze. Cut a hole in the middle for steam to escape. Stand the dish on the preheated baking sheet and bake for 45 minutes or until the pastry is golden brown. Transfer to a wire rack and leave to stand for 15 minutes before eating.

ROAST BELLY PORK WITH ASPARAGUS & RED PEPPER SALAD

I hesitate to offer something that might appear almost too simple to constitute a recipe, but then I think no, this dish really gets to the heart of the belly and makes it taste better than you have ever imagined it could. I've cooked belly pork for years – mainly slowly, in the pot, breathing spice and fruit as it stews. Here, the initial searingly hot roasting turns the crackling so salty-crisp you can tap it with a knife and it almost shatters like glass. Four hours slow cooking leaves the meat succulent, tender and basted in its own juices. (*Also illustrated on previous page*)

serves 4

1–1.2kg piece belly pork, scored
sea salt and black pepper
1 head of new season's garlic, cloves separated but not peeled
a glass of dry vermouth, white wine or cider

for the salad
4 Romano or other red peppers, halved, cored and deseeded
3–4 tbsp olive oil
4 good-quality anchovies, rinsed and drained
450g asparagus, trimmed, woody ends snapped off
grated zest of 1 lemon and a spritz of juice
2 heaped tbsp coarsely chopped flat-leaf parsley

Preheat the oven to 180°C/Gas 4. Lay the pork belly, rind up, on a board and sprinkle liberally with salt, set aside. Place the pepper halves for the salad, skin side down, in a roasting tin, sprinkle with ½ tbsp olive oil and a little salt and roast for 30 minutes until soft and browning at the edges. Place in a bowl, cover and leave to cool slightly, then peel away the skin and cut the peppers into strips.

Turn the oven up to 220°C/Gas 7. Place the pork belly in a roasting tin and roast for 45 minutes until the crackling is crisp all over. Take out of the oven and lower the setting to 130°C/Gas ½. Stab the sharp point of a small knife in between the crackling and meat at intervals, to release more fat. Add the garlic cloves (skin on), and roll them round in the fat. Cook for a further 4 hours at this low temperature, stabbing with the knife to release more fat every hour or so if you remember. The crackling will stay crisp while the meat slowly tenderises. Keep draining off the fat every hour too.

Half an hour or so before the pork will be ready, prepare the salad. Mash the anchovies on a plate with ½ tbsp olive oil. Slice the asparagus on the diagonal. Heat 2 tbsp olive oil in a heavy-bottomed frying pan and sauté the asparagus with a little salt for 8–10 minutes until tender when tested with a knife. Add the mashed anchovies, then take off the heat. Sprinkle in the lemon zest and juice with some pepper, then taste and adjust the seasoning. Tip into a bowl, add the pepper strips with the parsley and toss together so the flavours marry, adding a little more olive oil if needed. Let stand for 10 minutes.

Lift the cooked pork belly onto a board and leave to rest in a warm place for 10 minutes. Meanwhile, drain off the fat from the roasting tin, retaining the meat juices and garlic. Mash the garlic into the juices, then place over a medium heat. Splosh over the alcohol and bring to a bubble, scraping up the sediment. Strain into a warm jug. Carve the pork and serve with the gravy, salad and new potatoes.

BOILED BACON IN PERRY WITH CABBAGE & CASHEL BLUE

Every summer we take the ferry to Ireland and drive like hell for 6 hours to the west. We arrive in Co Mayo to be greeted with a traditional first night dinner by my neighbour Mary: boiled bacon and cabbage. No less of a treat for being annual and expected, a ritual. It was when I dined at The Old Convent at Clogheen in Tipperary at the hands of a brilliant young chef, Dermot Gannon, that the dish reached new heights. There was a twang of blue cheese scenting his buttery ribbons of cabbage. How brilliantly yet subtly blue cheese works with pork. Use any blue you have to hand, but none too salt with bacon. Perry (cider made with pears) marries beautifully with bacon too, but you can use cider if you wish. The accompanying dish of butter beans can be made the day before and is even lovelier reheated when all the flavours have got to know one another.

serves 6–8

1.6kg bacon joint
1 onion, peeled and spiked with 2 cloves
2 x 500ml bottles perry (pear cider)
6 black peppercorns
1 tsp cloves, crushed
1 tsp allspice, crushed
1 tbsp Dijon mustard
1 tbsp grainy mustard
1 tbsp dark molasses sugar

for the cabbage
1 green cabbage
60g butter
2 shallots, peeled and finely chopped
1 garlic clove, peeled and finely chopped
1 thyme sprig
a glass of Riesling or other medium, dry white wine
4 tbsp double cream
60–90g blue cheese, such as Cashel Blue
sea salt and black pepper

Put the bacon into a cooking pot with the clove-spiked onion, pour over the perry and throw in the peppercorns. Bring to the boil, put the lid on, lower the heat and simmer gently on the hob for an hour (or in the oven preheated to 180°C/Gas 4 if you prefer).

Lift the bacon joint out of the pot and place in a roasting tin; save a ladleful of the liquor. Switch the oven to 200°C/Gas 6. Using the point of a sharp knife, score through the skin and fat in a criss-cross fashion, just through to the meat. Mix the cloves, allspice, mustards and molasses sugar together and spoon on top of the bacon, pressing it down into the slashes. Bake in the oven for around 20 minutes until brown and bubbling, spooning the black sticky juices back over the bacon a few times. Rest for 10 minutes before carving.

Once the glazed bacon is in the oven, prepare the cabbage. Slice into fine ribbons and set aside. Melt half the butter in a wide pan and sweat the shallots, garlic and thyme until starting to soften. Splash in the wine, turn up the heat and let bubble to reduce a little, then add the reserved ladleful of bacon liquor. Bubble to reduce by about two-thirds, then add the cream and reduce until the sauce is fairly thick.

Meanwhile melt the rest of the butter in another pan, add the cabbage and cook over a high heat for 4–5 minutes until still crunchy, then drain off all the liquid. Pour in the sauce, crumble in the cheese and heat for a couple of minutes until it has melted, turning the cabbage to coat in the sauce. Taste and adjust the seasoning. You may wish to add a little more cheese, but I prefer a subtle hint of blue.

Serve with the butter beans, a pot of seeded mustard and mashed potato if you like – I can never resist.

BUTTER BEANS WITH FENNEL, OLIVES & SAVORY

Soak 450g dried butter beans overnight in cold water. Drain and put into a large heavy-bottomed pan with 1 onion stuck with 2 cloves, 2 chopped celery stalks, 3 chopped carrots, a few black peppercorns and a bouquet of fresh bay, rosemary, thyme and parsley (but no salt). Bring to the boil, skim, then put the lid on and simmer until tender, 1½–2 hours depending on the age of the beans. Drain, retaining a ladleful of the cooking liquor; discard the vegetables.

Shortly before the beans will be cooked, steam 2 trimmed and quartered fennel bulbs until *al dente,* about 7 minutes. Heat 2 tbsp olive oil in a frying pan, add 2 sliced garlic cloves and sauté briefly, then scatter over 1 tbsp chopped summer savory or 2 tsp chopped thyme leaves and 1 heaped tbsp coarsely chopped black olives. Swirl in 4 tbsp cream, then add the fennel and reheat briefly. Tip the contents of the pan into the beans and stir gently, so as not to break them up. Season to taste, allowing for the saltiness of the bacon.

SUMMER SKIRT WITH CHIMICHURRI & CORN-UTOPIA SALSA

There is nothing cheap, in the pejorative sense of the word, about a piece of summer skirt. It is what the French call 'onglet' or flank steak, so whilst not as tender or highly prized as rump, sirloin or fillet, it is perfect for the griddle or barbecue, and staggeringly cheap. I simply slice it thinly across the grain once it has rested. Smoky with picante pimentón, daughter no.1 Miranda's chimichurri echoes the scent of barbecue smoke. A dish to eat hot, warm or at room or garden temperature.

serves 4

1 thick piece of skirt, about 600g
sea salt and black pepper
a little olive oil

for the chimichurri
small bunch of flat-leaf parsley, chopped
1 medium red onion, peeled and finely chopped
4 garlic cloves, peeled and crushed
½ red pepper, deseeded and diced, or 4 roasted piquillo peppers from a jar, drained and diced
1 tomato, peeled, deseeded and finely chopped
1 tbsp chopped oregano leaves
1 tsp smoked paprika (or ordinary paprika)
1 tsp shredded bay leaf (in very small flakes)
1 tsp coarse sea salt
1 tsp ground black pepper
a knife tip of dried chilli flakes, to taste
50ml water
100ml olive oil
50ml red wine vinegar

corn-utopia salsa
2 corn-on-the-cobs
3–4 large tomatoes
1 small red onion, peeled and finely diced
small bunch of coriander, chopped
grated zest and juice of 1 lime
1 tbsp olive oil

First make the chimichurri. Mix all the ingredients, except the olive oil and wine vinegar, together in a large bowl, tossing well. Leave to stand for 30 minutes to allow the flavours to marry.

Meanwhile, for the salsa, cook the corn cobs in boiling salted water until tender, about 15 minutes. Slice the corn kernels off the cobs and tip them into a bowl. Immerse the tomatoes in a bowl of boiling hot water for 30 seconds, then drain, refresh under cold water and peel. Halve, deseed and dice the tomatoes. Add to the corn with the rest of the ingredients. Season with salt and pepper to taste and stir gently to combine.

Heat up your barbecue or brush a griddle or heavy cast-iron pan with a little olive oil and heat until starting to smoke. Season one side of the skirt and place it, seasoned side down, on the griddle. Cook for about 4 minutes, then season the surface, flip the steak over and cook for another 4 minutes. The meat should now be medium-rare. To check, press with your fingers before removing from the griddle; it should be springy to the touch. Transfer to a carving board, cover loosely with foil and leave to rest for 5 minutes.

Meanwhile, stir the oil and wine vinegar into the chimichurri. Using a well-sharpened carving knife, slice the beef very thinly, horizontally across the grain, and lay on a warmed large platter. (If, as you carve, the meat looks a bit raw towards the middle, simply put it back on the griddle for a minute).

Drizzle some of the chimichurri across the meat. Put the rest into a small serving bowl for guests to help themselves. Accompany with the corn-utopia salsa.

CALF'S CHEEKS IN GRAINY MUSTARD WITH ROSEMARY

In bad times and good we still want to eat well. All that changes is the amount we have to spend on food, we have to cook more creatively with ingredients that we may be unfamiliar with.

This is the year of the 'chap', a sixteenth century word for a chop, meaning the cheeks and jaws of an animal. Ox cheeks have a heartier flavour than the younger, subtler, paler more sticky-sweet glueiness of calves, whose flesh is more delicate. The flavour needs bolstering and encouraging with the same things you would use with veal – rosemary, sherry, carrot, celery and grainy mustard You do not want the delicate to seem robust though, so I capture the essence without overdoing it.

This recipe has been tried and tested with ox cheeks too, which may be easier to find at your butcher.

serves 4

4 calf's cheeks
flour, to coat
sea salt and black pepper
2 tbsp olive oil
1 rosemary sprig, 7–8cm long, leaves stripped and finely chopped
2 red onions, peeled and chopped
2 celery stalks, de-strung with a potato peeler and chopped
4 carrots, peeled and cut into chunks on the diagonal
a glass of Oloroso sherry (or Fino, Madeira or Marsala)
2 tsp grainy mustard
⅓ bottle red wine, warmed

Preheat the oven to 140°C/Gas 1. Trim the calf's cheeks if necessary. Season the flour with salt and pepper and turn the cheeks in it to coat all over.

Heat the olive oil in a heavy-bottomed flameproof casserole and add the rosemary, letting it fizz and pop for a minute. Add the calf's cheeks and brown for a good 5 minutes on each side, adding a little more seasoning. Remove to a plate.

Add the onions, celery and carrots to the casserole and fry gently for 10 minutes until they begin to soften. Return the meat to the casserole, pour in the sherry and let it reduce right down, then stir in the mustard. Add the warmed wine and bring to a simmer.

Cover the surface closely with a circle of greaseproof paper cut to fit (a cartouche) and a lid and cook in the oven for 2½ hours or until the cheeks are soft and yielding when pierced with a skewer.

Serve with spring cabbage or a dark, leafy vegetable and plenty of mashed potato.

FILLET OF VENISON (OR LAMB) WITH A SPICED AUBERGINE CHARLOTTE

Game time. Wild venison is in a league of its own, the depth of flavour and gameyness is incomparable. But for those of you who don't live in the backwoods or have your own dealer, buy farmed venison. Red-blooded red deer, that's what I like, and the spiced aubergine matches it flavour for flavour. When you turn out the charlotte with its pretty tongues of aubergine furled around the spiced tomato sauce – like a happy cat with a saucer of cream – you will exclaim, congratulate yourself, take heart at how easily something so very out of the ordinary has been accomplished.

The venison fillet needs your attention for 12–15 minutes, as it is cooked in a pan last minute, but the ritual of turning the meat and letting it rest while you deglaze the pan and concoct a simple, syrupy, berried and boozed sauce is straightforward and not technically for the master chefs.

If you can't get or don't like venison, fillet of lamb would be lovely; it too has an affinity with the aubergine.

serves 4

600–675g piece of venison fillet, red deer if possible and wild
sea salt
2 tbsp olive oil, plus extra to rub
14–16 juniper berries, crushed
about 12 black peppercorns, cracked
a wine glass of Marsala
2 tsp crab apple, redcurrant or rowan jelly
1 tbsp crème de myrtilles, mûres or cassis
a few little knobs of butter

for the aubergine charlotte
2 aubergines
2–3 tbsp olive oil
1 large onion, peeled and finely chopped
1 celery stalk, de-strung with a potato peeler and finely chopped
2 garlic cloves, peeled and finely chopped
1 generous tsp ground turmeric
1 generous tsp garam masala
¼ tsp dried chilli flakes
5 crushed cloves
1 tsp ground cinnamon
2 tsp chopped thyme leaves
12 large tomatoes, coarsely chopped

Preheat the oven to 200°C/Gas 6. For the charlotte, slice the aubergines vertically into slim tongues, ideally using a mandolin. Lay them on an oiled baking tray, sprinkle with olive oil and bake for 7 minutes or until softened right through. Transfer to a large plate.

Heat 2 tbsp olive oil in a heavy-bottomed frying pan. Add the onion and celery with a pinch of salt and cook for a few minutes until starting to soften and turn translucent, then toss in the garlic. Stir in the spices and thyme and cook, stirring frequently, for 5 minutes before adding the tomatoes. Cover and cook for 20 minutes, then remove the lid and simmer for 15–20 minutes until the sauce is thick.

Grease a 900ml soufflé dish. Line with overlapping tongues of aubergine, leaving some overhanging the rim of the dish. Spoon in the spiced tomato sauce and fold the overhanging aubergine slices over the top, adding more to cover so that the sauce is entirely cloaked like a parcel. (You can hold the dish for a few hours at this point, or keep it in the fridge and bring it back to room temperature before you cook it.) Cover tightly with foil and stand the soufflé dish in a roasting tin. Surround with boiling water to come halfway up the sides of the dish. Cook in the oven for 35 minutes.

About 20 minutes before you wish to serve, season the venison with salt, rub all over with olive oil and sprinkle with the crushed juniper and cracked pepper. Heat 2 tbsp olive oil in a heavy-bottomed frying pan large enough to contain the venison. Lay the fillet in the pan and brown it on one side for 5 minutes. Turn over and repeat. The meat should be brown all round but rare in the middle. Remove to a board, unless you wish to take it further, but it will be juicy, tender and flavoursome if cooked to this point. Cover loosely with foil and leave to rest in a warm place while you make the sauce.

Once the charlotte is cooked, leave it to stand for a few minutes before turning out onto a large plate.

Deglaze the venison pan quickly over a lively heat with the Marsala. Add the fruit jelly and liqueur and let it bubble hard before introducing the knobs of butter to turn the sauce glossy and velvety.

Using a serrated knife, cut the charlotte into wedges. Carve the venison into thick slices, arrange on warm plates and pour some of the sauce over. Place a wedge of aubergine charlotte and a portion of the potatoes (see below) alongside.

POMMES ANNA

Sticky with chicken stock but not rich like a Dauphinois, this is the ideal accompaniment here. It's simply peeled, washed and patted-dry potatoes, sliced very thinly and built up in seasoned layers in a buttered gratin dish, with hot chicken stock poured on to come three-quarters of the way up the potatoes. I drop a few knobs of butter on top with the final seasoning, cover with foil and cook on the hob for 5 minutes to get it going. Then it's in the oven at 200°C/Gas 6 for 50 minutes. To brown the top, remove the foil and cook for a further 10–15 minutes. Check the potatoes are cooked by piercing with a skewer.

MAQLUBA

'Maqluba', an Arab dish from the Levant, means 'upside down', so it is the tatin of the savoury world in Palestine and something of a show-stopper despite its unshowy ingredients. In the thirteenth century book, *A Baghdad Cookery Book*, there is a whole chapter devoted to 'fried, marinated and turned' dishes. But no inverting snobbery here: flipping tarts or upside down cakes, steamed puddings or maqlubas, creates a sense of occasion; a sleight of hand at the table is met with a gasp of awe as the dish makes contact with the plate and what lies beneath is revealed, ready to strew with flaked almonds, pine nuts, parsley and mint.

serves 4

180g brown basmati rice
1 tsp ground turmeric
2 large aubergines
5–6 tbsp olive oil
450g minced lamb or good pork sausages, skinned and crumbled
1 tsp freshly ground allspice
½ tsp ground cinnamon
a suspicion of freshly grated nutmeg
2–3 thyme sprigs, leaves stripped and chopped
2 garlic cloves, peeled and sliced
sea salt and black pepper
2 onions, peeled and thinly sliced
450g courgettes (ideally a mix of yellow and green), sliced lengthways
120g Puy or red lentils
4 large tomatoes, sliced, or 24 whole cherry tomatoes
600ml hot chicken stock
30g pine nuts or flaked almonds (or a mixture), lightly toasted
1 tbsp chopped flat-leaf parsley
1 tbsp chopped mint

Tip the rice into a bowl, add the turmeric and pour on sufficient water to cover, then leave to soak for an hour. Preheat the oven to 190°C/Gas 5. Cut the aubergines into slices, the thickness of a £1 coin. Brush them with olive oil on both sides and lay on a large baking sheet. Bake in the oven for 15–20 minutes until tender.

Meanwhile, put the mince or sausage into a bowl and add the spices, thyme, garlic, ½ tsp salt and a good scrunch of pepper. Mix thoroughly with your hands until evenly combined.

Heat 2 tbsp olive oil in a large frying pan, add the meat and stir over a medium-high heat until evenly browned. Tip out onto a plate; set aside. Add a little more oil to the pan, then cook the onions and courgettes gently until soft and translucent. Remove from the heat.

Drain the rice thoroughly and toss with the lentils. Oil a tatin pan or large gratin dish and arrange a layer of tomatoes on the bottom. Layer half of the rice and lentils on top and cover with half of the aubergines. Add the spiced meat in a layer, followed by the onions and courgettes, the remaining aubergines and finally the rest of the rice and lentils.

Pour on three-quarters of the hot stock, cover and bake for 40 minutes, then add the rest of the stock, re-cover and return to the oven for a further 20 minutes or until the rice is cooked through.

Invert the maqluba onto a warmed large plate and sprinkle with the toasted nuts. Scatter the chopped parsley and mint over the surface and serve.

ROAST LAMB WITH FLAMED PEPPERS, SHERRY & SPANISH RICE

I wanted a Sunday lunch with a difference, something with Spanish overtones, charred and creamed Romano peppers, Spanish rice spiked with sherry and garlic, the lamb pasted with paprika and fresh rosemary. This is it. It was ravenously approved.

serves 6

1 leg of lamb, about 1.6kg
2 fat garlic cloves, peeled
sea salt and black pepper
1 tsp paprika
2 tbsp olive oil
a bushy sprig of rosemary, leaves stripped and very finely chopped
1 large onion, peeled and thinly sliced
150ml dry sherry (Fino or Amontillado)

for the peppers

8 Romano or other red peppers
3–4 tbsp double cream
½ tsp sugar

for the rice

2 tbsp olive oil
1 red onion, peeled and chopped
2 fat garlic cloves, peeled and finely sliced
2 thyme sprigs, leaves stripped and chopped
400g Calasparra or brown basmati rice
225ml sherry (Fino or Amontillado)
1 litre hot chicken stock
pinch of cayenne pepper
2 tbsp pine nuts, lightly toasted (optional)
2 tbsp flaked almonds, lightly toasted (optional)

Preheat the oven to 200°C/Gas 6. Place the lamb on a board. Crush the garlic with a little salt, then tip into a bowl and stir in the paprika, olive oil and chopped rosemary. Spike slits in the fat layer covering the lamb with the point of a knife. Rub the garlicky paste over the meat, pushing it down into the cuts.

Scatter the onion slices in a roasting tin and place the leg of lamb on top. Roast for about 1½ hours or until a skewer pierces easily through the flesh and the emerging juices run pink, not raw and bloody looking.

While the lamb is roasting, prepare the peppers and rice. Grill the peppers or scorch them by turning on a fork over a gas flame, until charred on all sides. Put into a bowl, cover with cling film and leave for 20 minutes; the steam will help to lift the skins. Peel away the skins, halve the peppers lengthways and remove the seeds, then place on a plate with any juices. Transfer all but 2 pepper halves to a gratin dish, cover and keep warm in a low oven.

Put the two pepper halves into a blender with all the pepper juices, the cream, sugar and some salt and pepper. Blitz to a sauce. Tip into a small pan and set aside.

For the rice, heat the olive oil in a heavy-bottomed casserole, add the onion and fry gently until softened and translucent. Add the garlic and thyme and sauté for a minute or two, then tip in the rice and stir to coat the grains in oil. Pour in two-thirds of the sherry and let it bubble almost all away, then add the hot stock, cayenne and some salt and pepper. Bring to the boil, turn down to a simmer, put the lid on and cook until *al dente*; allow 20 minutes for Calasparra, a little longer for brown basmati (be guided by the packet directions).

When the rice is ready, remove the pan from the heat. Add the rest of the sherry, fork through and put the lid back on. Leave to stand for 10 minutes.

Once the lamb is cooked, transfer it to a carving board, cover loosely with foil and leave to rest in a warm spot for about 15 minutes while you prepare the gravy.

Put the roasting tin over a medium-high heat, splash in the sherry and stir to scrape up the sediment and mix with the caramelised onions. Cook until browned and bubbling, adding any cooking water from accompanying veg. Strain this gravy into a jug, tipping in any meat juices from the resting lamb.

Warm the pepper cream gently in the small pan and then pour over the peppers. Transfer the rice to a warmed bowl and scatter with the toasted nuts, if using. Cut the lamb into thick chunks (rather than thin slices).

Serve the lamb chunks on top of the rice, with two pepper halves alongside and some creamed pepper spooned on top of the meat. Accompany with the gravy and vegetables of your choice.

SPICY LAMB KOFTE WITH TAHINI YOGHURT & HONEY MISO SAUCE

The spices come out with the sun. We tend to rub our meat before we slash and burn, flay the flesh on griddle and grills and coals, enhancing it with something sturdy enough, man enough to cope with the scent of the charcoal, the wood, the smoke.

Either that, or we leave the meat plain and unadulterated but for a little seasoning and oil and then introduce a vibrant sauce to dip the meat into. Something savoury, piquant, full of vigour.

The miso sauce works equally well with pork, so substitute pork for lamb if it suits you, or with beef if you want the trad burger. You can make patties or bamboo skewers of the meat and either barbecue it, griddle it, stick it under the grill, or put it in the oven. The timing will be different for each type of meat and according to your preference for pink or well-cooked lamb or beef.

serves 4

450g minced lamb
1 small onion, peeled and finely chopped
2 tbsp chopped mint leaves
1 tsp chopped thyme leaves
2 large garlic cloves, peeled and crushed
2 tsp ground coriander
2 tsp ground cumin
1 tsp ground caraway seeds
½ tsp ground chilli flakes
1 tsp sea salt
1 tsp cracked black peppercorns (or coarsely ground will do)
1 tbsp strong-flavoured runny honey (such as chestnut)

Presoak 8 long bamboo skewers in water to prevent them from scorching on the barbecue or under the grill. Simply put all the kofte ingredients into a large bowl and mix thoroughly with your hands. (Don't use a food processor, if you do the mince will lose its texture and turn into an unappetising sludge.)

Form the mixture into 8 bullrush shapes and skewer them on the bamboo skewers. Set aside on a plate until you are ready to cook.

Heat up the barbecue or an oiled griddle. Cook the kofte for 8–10 minutes, turning them every couple of minutes. If you prefer browned lamb to juicy pink, cook them for a further 5 minutes or so. (I have also cooked them in a hot oven at 200°C/Gas 6 on a rack over a roasting tin for 15 minutes, turning at half time.) In the heat of the summer, rest the lamb for 20 minutes or so before serving, so it is not piping hot.

Serve the kofte with one or both of the sauces (opposite) and a refreshing cucumber, tomato and mint salad dressed with olive oil and lemon juice.

TAHINI YOGHURT SAUCE

Put 250g Greek organic bio yoghurt into a serving bowl and crush a large garlic clove into it. Stir in 1½–2 tsp dark tahini (sesame seed paste) and season with salt and pepper. Taste and adjust; you do not want the sesame flavour to overwhelm the sauce. Sprinkle 1 tbsp chopped mint leaves over the sauce and serve with the lamb kofte.

HONEY MISO SAUCE

Simply whisk 2 tbsp miso paste, 2 tbsp runny honey, 1 tbsp Dijon mustard, 2 crushed large garlic cloves, 2 tbsp grated fresh root ginger, 2 tbsp tamari or shoyu sauce and 1½ tbsp cider vinegar together in bowl and use as a dipping sauce for the kofte.

NOTE

I often cook a leg of lamb in this miso sauce, first inserting slices of garlic into slits in the fat, then rubbing garam masala all over the surface. I spoon the honey miso sauce over the meat, then roast it in the normal way, adding a small mug of water to the miso juices in the roasting tin halfway through. Once the lamb has rested, I serve it sliced with the blackened juices spooned over and a bowl of tahini yoghurt sauce on the side.

TURKEY KOFTE

Free-range turkey mince is increasingly visible on the summer meat counter and is a delish alternative, if pepped up, to lamb or pork kofte. It does need feisty flavourings to alleviate the bland, which the chilli, garam masala and mustard have in spadefuls. The good thing about the meat is that it is succulent and fatty enough to press onto the bamboo sticks and barbecue or griddle without drying out. Please use chicken, veal, pork, lamb or beef mince if they suit you better. The main point here is the balance of spice and herb, and not having meat too lean for its own good.

serves 4

500g free-range turkey mince
1 tbsp finely chopped coriander leaves
1 tbsp finely chopped mint leaves
2 tsp Dijon mustard
2 tsp garam masala
1 tbsp olive oil
a finger of fresh root ginger, coarsely grated, skin on
1 large garlic clove, peeled and crushed
sea salt and black pepper
½ tsp dried chilli flakes

Presoak 8 long bamboo skewers in water (to prevent them scorching). Simply mix all the ingredients together in a bowl with your hands and form into 8 bullrush shapes, pressing them onto long bamboo skewers and setting them aside on a plate until you are ready to cook them.

Heat up the barbecue or an oiled griddle. Cook the turkey kofte for about 2 minutes on each of the 4 sides, i.e. 8 minutes in total or until cooked right through.

Serve the kofte with a Middle Eastern diced cucumber, tomato and radish salad dressed with garlic, mint, lemon and olive oil, or a radish and spring onion raita (see below).

Accompany with buttery new potatoes or cardamom and turmeric spiced brown basmati rice.

RADISH & SPRING ONION RAITA

Put 250g Greek organic bio yoghurt into a serving bowl, crush a garlic clove into it and season with salt and pepper. Stir in 3–4 diced spring onions, 3–4 thinly sliced large radishes and ⅓ cucumber, peeled, deseeded and finely chopped. Scatter over a few shredded mint leaves and add a sprinkling of black onion seeds too, if you wish.

STICKY HONEYED CHICKEN WINGS WITH ROASTED GARLIC AÏOLI

Stretching Sunday lunch, or any other meal, like a piece of elastic, is something I believe in firmly. Never say no to a last-minute guest, or two. It is not about apologising for the small amount of meat on the plate, it's about thinking creatively. This dish came about when the six chicken wings I'd bought for two suddenly needed to feed four. I charred peppers to make a salad with fresh goat's cheese and a heap of wild rocket, roasted new season's garlic and pounded it into an ointment of brilliant yellow aïoli to spoon over everything with baby Jersey new potatoes. The spread on the garden table looked like bounty, not like a scrimped and carefully managed affair.

serves 4

8–12 organic/free-range chicken wings or 4 large thighs
grated zest and juice of 1 lime
1 tbsp strong-flavoured runny honey (such as chestnut)
½ tsp dried chilli flakes
1 tsp chopped thyme leaves
1 tbsp good fruity olive oil
sea salt and black pepper

for the roasted garlic aïoli

a head of new season's garlic (or 4–6 raw garlic cloves later in the year)
olive oil, to dribble
2 egg yolks
150–250ml half groundnut/half mild olive oil

Put the chicken wings or thighs into a baking dish that will hold them in a single layer and spoon over the rest of the ingredients, seasoning to taste and turning the chicken to coat. Cover and leave to marinate in a cool place for an hour. Preheat the oven to 200°C/Gas 6.

Meanwhile, make the aïoli. Roast the garlic in a small roasting tin, with a little olive oil dribbled over, for 20 minutes. Turn and roast for another 20 minutes or until soft when pierced with a skewer. As soon as you can handle them, pop the garlic cloves out of their skins straight into a mortar and pound with the pestle. Add the egg yolks with some seasoning and pound to a smooth emulsion. Start adding the oil in a tiny but steady trickle as you stir and pound with the pestle, using your other hand. Stop when the aïoli is thick enough. Adjust the seasoning and if it isn't garlicky enough for you, add a crushed raw clove.

Spoon the marinade over the chicken again, then roast in the oven for 20 minutes. Turn the chicken, baste with the juices and roast for another 10 minutes, then baste again. The juices should now be dark and sticky. Cook wings for a final 5 minutes, thighs for 10 minutes or until cooked through. Serve with the aïoli and salad.

PEPPER, GOAT'S CHEESE & WILD ROCKET SALAD

Grill 6 Romano or other peppers, or scorch by turning on a fork over a gas flame, until charred on all sides. Put in a bowl, cover with cling film and leave until just cool enough to handle, then peel away the skins, deseed and cut the peppers into strips. For the dressing, shake 1 tbsp balsamic or sherry vinegar, 4 tbsp olive oil and some seasoning in a screw-topped jar. While still warm, toss the peppers with the dressing, a bunch of wild rocket or watercress, a crumbled ½ small fresh goat's cheese and 1 tbsp each chopped parsley and coriander. The herbs will be softened and the flavours diffused by the warmth.

SAFFRON CHICKEN, LEEK & PRUNE PIE

Who doesn't love a home-made chicken pie? It is soul-food, if such a thing exists way away from its spiritual home in the Deep South. You need good chicken and good stock, made by cramming as many vegetables and herbs into the pot as you can. So how to spruce up the old familiar? By dint of a dearth. Saffron, leeks, tarragon and prunes invigorate the ivory tones of this classic dish and give it harmony and punch.

serves 6

1 organic/free-range chicken, about 1.8kg
flavouring vegetables, such as 2 onions spiked with 2 cloves, 2 chopped celery stalks, 2 carrots in chunks, cleaned green tops of 2 leeks
bunch of herbs, such as thyme, parsley, rosemary and 2 bay leaves, tied together
6 black peppercorns
stock or water to cover

for the sauce
good pinch of saffron stamens
60g unsalted butter
2 tbsp plain flour
about 300ml hot whole milk
sea salt and black pepper
a suspicion of freshly grated nutmeg
4 fat leeks with green tops, well washed and chopped
2 small onions, peeled and cut into eighths
1 heaped tbsp chopped tarragon
8–10 organic prunes, halved and stoned

for the pastry
180g plain flour
pinch of sea salt
90g chilled unsalted butter (or half butter, half lard), cut into cubes
1–1½ tbsp ice-cold water
1 egg yolk, beaten with 1 tsp milk, to glaze

Put the chicken, breast down, in a large cooking pot and add the flavouring vegetables, herbs and peppercorns. Pour over the stock or water, bring to the boil and skim the surface. Put the lid on and poach at a low simmer for an hour or until the chicken is cooked. Leave to cool in the pot with the lid off.

Meanwhile, soak the saffron in two ladlefuls of the hot poaching stock for 30 minutes. When the chicken is cool enough to handle, lift out of the pot and tear the meat off the bone into pieces, discarding the skin; set aside. Strain the stock (you'll need about 450ml).

To make the sauce, melt the butter in a pan, stir in the flour and cook for a minute to a pale biscuit coloured roux. Whisk in the saffron-infused stock. Now gradually whisk in the hot milk. Season and add a little nutmeg. Let simmer for 10 minutes, then throw in the leeks and onions. Bring to a simmer again, whisk in a couple more ladlefuls of stock, then cover and cook gently until the vegetables have softened. Stir in the tarragon and prunes. Taste and adjust the seasoning, and add a little more stock if you think it is needed. Remove from the heat, add the chicken, then tip the filling into your pie dish to cool.

To make the pastry, sift the flour and salt into a food processor, add the butter and pulse briefly to a crumb texture. Add 1 tbsp water and pulse just until the dough forms a ball, adding a little more water if needed. Wrap in cling film, flatten and chill for 30–45 minutes.

Preheat the oven to 180°C/Gas 4. Roll out the pastry on a lightly floured surface until larger all round than the pie dish. Brush the rim of the pie dish with water. Cut strips from the edge of the pastry and position on the rim. Stand a pie funnel in the centre of the dish, then drape the pastry lid over the dish. Trim the pastry edge, then press lightly with the tines of a fork to seal. Cut a cross above the funnel.

Brush the top with beaten egg and bake in the middle of the oven for 50 minutes or until the pastry is golden and the filling is bubbling; it may take another 10 minutes. Let stand for 10 minutes before serving.

CHICKEN TIKKA MASALA

A really good curry is the business, and top of the range has to be a chicken curry, intense with home-ground and tempered spices, served with fragrant saffron and cardamom rice, spiced dhal, home-made mango chutney (see page 183) and poppadums puffed up under the grill. Cook this chicken curry and pretty quickly your friends will arrive with crates of lager, demanding sitar music in your Indian kitchen. This dish is child-mild but you can go hot-hot with bird's eye chillies if you are so inclined.

serves 4

600g boned organic/free-range chicken thighs
3 tbsp light olive or groundnut oil
1 large onion, peeled and chopped
sea salt and black pepper
2 green chillies, deseeded and chopped
a thumb of fresh root ginger, peeled and grated
5 garlic cloves, peeled and finely chopped
¼ –½ tsp chilli powder
1½ tsp ground turmeric
2 tsp garam masala
2 tsp cumin seeds, toasted in a dry pan and ground
1 tbsp light muscovado sugar
1 tbsp tomato purée
400g tin chopped tomatoes
120ml hot chicken stock or water
10 fresh or dried curry leaves
200ml live yoghurt
2 tbsp double cream
1 tsp cornflour
2 tbsp roughly chopped coriander

Remove the skin from the chicken thighs, then cut them into bite-sized pieces and set aside.

Heat 2 tbsp of the oil in a large, heavy-bottomed frying pan, throw in the onion, sprinkle over a little salt and sauté gently for 15 minutes. Add the chopped chillies, ginger and garlic and cook for a further 2 minutes. Add the spices and cook, stirring, for a few minutes until fragrant, then tip out onto a plate.

Add the rest of the oil to the pan and brown the chicken pieces on both sides, in batches if necessary. Tip the spiced mixture back into the pan and add the sugar, tomato purée, tomatoes, hot stock or water and curry leaves. Grind over a little pepper, bring to the boil, then reduce to a simmer. Cover and cook for 20 minutes or until the chicken is tender and cooked through. Meanwhile, strain the yoghurt in a muslin-lined sieve.

When the chicken is cooked, remove the curry from the heat. Warm the cream in a small pan, mix in the cornflour and cook, stirring, for a minute, then remove from the heat and stir in the yoghurt (this should stop the sauce from splitting).

Stir the yoghurt into the chicken curry together with half of the chopped coriander.

Serve immediately, sprinkled with the rest of the coriander.

CHICKEN & MUSHROOM BREAST POCKETS

This is a dish perfectly temperamentally suited to tardy guests or early prep and later finishing off. The mushroom, mustard, mascarpone and vermouth stuffing elevates it from the commonplace to Friday- or any other-night special. It is a dish of elegant simplicity and depth of flavour and wholly uncomplicated to make.

serves 6

6 organic/free-range chicken breasts, skin on
sea salt and black pepper
2 tbsp olive oil
30g butter
1 small red onion, peeled and finely chopped
250g crimini or chestnut mushrooms, wiped clean and thinly sliced
1 garlic clove, peeled and crushed
2 tsp chopped oregano leaves
1 tsp chopped thyme leaves
4–6 tbsp dry vermouth
2 tsp Dijon mustard
2 tbsp mascarpone

Season the chicken breasts all over with salt and pepper. Heat the olive oil in a heavy-bottomed frying pan until almost smoking, then add the seasoned chicken breasts, skin-side down, and fry for about 5 minutes until browned. Turn the chicken breasts over and fry a little more gently for a couple of minutes, then remove the pan from the heat. Leave to cool down.

In another frying pan, melt the butter and, when it begins to foam, add the onion and mushrooms. Fry until the mushrooms begin to exude their juices, then continue to cook until the juices have reduced and only a little remains. Add the garlic and herbs, stir briefly and then splosh over half the vermouth. Let it bubble and reduce by about two-thirds, then add the rest of the vermouth. As it begins to bubble, stir in the mustard and mascarpone. Cook for another 5 minutes, season with salt and pepper to taste and remove from the heat. Leave to cool.

Preheat the oven to 190°C/Gas 5. Cut the chicken breasts horizontally almost in two, so you can open them out like a book. Stuff with the mushroom mixture and close them. Lay the stuffed chicken breasts in a single layer in an ovenproof heavy-bottomed pan or gratin dish, placing them close together.

Bake in the oven for 25–30 minutes, or until the juices run clear when the thickest part of the breasts is pierced through with a skewer. They will have created delicious juices to spoon over them.

Serve with roasted sweet potato wedges and mangetout, sugar snaps or buttered spring cabbage to add greenness and crunch.

CHICKEN TANGIA WITH SMOKED AUBERGINE & RED PEPPER COUSCOUS

The tangia is an untemperamental yet feisty dish, emboldened with the colour and fragrance of the Middle East. The preserved lemon gives it tang and the couscous is enlivened with fresh herbs, aubergine and grilled peppers. If you do not have a whole chicken or simply want to be more economical, make the dish with chicken thighs. Prepare the chicken ahead and reheat, if it suits you better to cook early and eat late.

I cook a whole packet of couscous, because any that's left over is great spruced up as a salad the following day. Just add more olive oil, an extra tsp of harissa if you like it hot, more toasted cumin, a handful of chick peas or lentils and some freshly chopped herbs – parsley, mint, coriander – whatever you have.

serves 6

1 organic/free-range chicken, about 1.6kg, jointed, legs and breasts halved
2 preserved lemons
1 large onion, peeled and coarsely chopped
6 garlic cloves, peeled and halved
4 tbsp olive oil
1½ tbsp cumin seeds, toasted and crushed
3 tbsp chopped coriander
generous pinch of saffron stamens, soaked in 3–4 tbsp hot water for 20 minutes
30g unsalted butter, in pieces
sea salt and black pepper

for the couscous
1 aubergine
1 each red and yellow peppers (or both red)
500g packet couscous
600ml warm water
3–4 tbsp light olive oil
2 tbsp chopped coriander leaves, or 1 tbsp each chopped coriander and flat-leaf parsley
1 tbsp chopped mint leaves

to serve
harissa (see right)

Make deep slashes through the chicken skin into the flesh and then place in a shallow earthenware baking dish. Halve the lemons and remove all the pips, then put into a food processor with the onion, garlic, olive oil, 1 tbsp of the toasted cumin and the chopped coriander. Blitz to a rough paste; don't over-process.

Spread the paste over the chicken and work into the slashes with your fingers. Sprinkle over the saffron and its water and dot with the butter. Leave to marinate for 4–6 hours if time, otherwise 30 minutes will do.

Preheat the oven to 180°C/Gas 4. Cover the dish with foil, sealing it tightly, and cook in the oven for 50 minutes or until the chicken is cooked through. Taste and adjust the seasoning.

Meanwhile, for the couscous, prick the aubergine in a few places with the tip of a knife. Grill or hold with tongs over a gas flame, turning until charred all over and cooked through. This should take about 5 minutes, but test with a skewer. Put the aubergine into a large bowl and cover with cling film. Do the same with the peppers, adding them to the aubergine. Leave, tightly covered, to steam in the residual heat for 20 minutes, then peel away the skins. Core and deseed the peppers, saving their juice, then slice into strips. Chop the aubergine and mash a little. Set both aside on separate plates.

Put the couscous into a large bowl with 1 tsp salt. Pour on the warm water and stir to ensure the couscous absorbs the water evenly, then leave to plump up a little for 10 minutes.

Add 2 tbsp olive oil and sift the couscous grains between your hands, rubbing them as you do so to prevent clumps forming. Wrap the couscous in a piece of muslin, place in a steamer and steam for

10 minutes. (Alternatively, you can cook the plumped couscous in a foil-covered dish in the oven with your tangia for 20 minutes.)

Sprinkle the couscous with the remaining olive oil and the rest of the toasted cumin. Riffle through the grain with your fingers and a fork to keep them separate. Toss through most of the herbs.

Tip the couscous into a large, hot serving dish and gently fork through the smoky aubergine. Top with the grilled pepper strips.

Serve the chicken straight from the cooking dish, with the couscous, harissa and Moroccan carrots – a lovely accompaniment. You can pour some of the fragrant chicken liquor over the couscous to keep it well lubricated. If you like a hot dish, add a ladleful of the juices to 1 level tbsp of the harissa and stir together, then anoint the fiery sauce over your couscous. Otherwise, serve the harissa in a separate bowl so that guests may choose whatever degree of heat suits them.

HARISSA

Put 85g piquillo peppers from a jar or 1 skinned roasted red pepper in a blender with 4 medium-hot red chillies or 2 bird's eye hot chillies (you decide), 3 tsp ground toasted cumin seeds, 4 peeled garlic cloves, 1 tbsp tomato purée, 2 tsp red wine vinegar, 2 tsp smoked paprika, 4 tbsp olive oil and some sea salt and black pepper. Blend to a paste. Taste and adjust the seasoning and heat level as you wish. Store in a jar, covered with a thin film of olive oil, in the fridge and use within a couple of weeks. You can stir the olive oil into the harissa before using. Use leftover harissa to pep up soups and stews; it's also great in a toasted cheese sandwich.

MOROCCAN CARROTS

Cut 500g carrots into thick chunks on the diagonal, tip into a saucepan and add just enough water to cover. Add 4 peeled garlic cloves and a little sea salt and cook until tender but not soft. Drain and return to the pan, picking out the garlic. Crush the garlic cloves and scatter over the carrots in the pan. Add 4 tbsp olive oil, 2 tbsp cider vinegar, 1 tsp each crushed, toasted cumin and coriander seeds, ½ tsp each smoked paprika and chilli flakes and 1 tbsp coarsely chopped coriander. Toss for a few seconds over the heat and then transfer to a warmed serving bowl. Sprinkle with more chopped coriander and serve hot or warm.

SWEET THINGS

There are pudding people and there are non-pudding people, a race that may, as far as I am concerned, come from a planet at the far arm of a galaxy a trillion miles away, an alter-universe.

How could you not delight in a luscious lemon cake, a vibrant pomegranate sorbet or a goddess of an Aphrodite's pudding? Or pucker a lip with a sharp passion fruit sorbet or drizzle-drenched cake? Does a killer black and white chocolate cake not raise a smile? Does an old-fashioned Italian torta della nonna, the grandmother of tarts, with its lemon-peel scented custard and toasted pine nuts, not invite you to indulge?

Even if you think you are too lazy to make a pudding, the chocolate and morello cherry fridge cake should have you chopping in seconds; it takes longer to read the instructions than it does to make, and for some, there is no incentive more appealing.

The pomegranate sorbet is a jewelled delicacy, the summer berry génoise gaudy and gorgeous, a thing that will define your summer. Once made, you will go back to it again and again. Berried brilliance oozing with an airily light filling and sponge. A sense of wickedness and extravagance, but without the cream and butter that turns gâteau to guilt. Irresistible. On my planet.

BRIOCHE & BUTTER PUDDING WITH STRAWBERRY JAM

There is no end to what we can do with stale crumb: of cake or bread, pannetone or hot cross bun, bathing in a canary-yellow custard infused with vanilla and laced with dried fruit soaked in anything much you fancy, from sherry to rum to orange juice. The secret of this pudding is to butter and jam the bottom layer of brioche but butter only the top before baking. Once it comes bubbling out of the oven, brush the top deck with the last of the jam and bring it glistening to the table.

serves 6–8

½ shop-bought, 2–3-day-old all-butter brioche loaf, or 6 brioche rolls
300ml whole milk (ideally Jersey)
300ml double cream (ideally Jersey)
1 vanilla pod, split, seeds scraped out
3 eggs, plus 2 egg yolks
90g vanilla caster sugar
60g or so butter, melted
375g jar good strawberry jam with whole berries (I use Little Scarlet)
2 tsp water

Slice the brioche loaf, or split rolls in two if using. Preheat the oven to 180°C/Gas 4. Pour the milk and cream into a saucepan, add the vanilla pod and seeds and heat slowly, almost to the boil. Meanwhile, whisk the eggs, egg yolks and sugar together thoroughly in a large bowl. Pour on the hot creamy milk, whisking well. Remove the vanilla pod (save it for your vanilla sugar jar).

Arrange half of the brioche in a layer in a buttered baking dish and brush with melted butter. Gently melt half the strawberry jam with 1 tsp water and pour over the buttered brioche slices, brushing to coat all over. Arrange the rest of the brioche on top, brush with the remaining butter and then pour the custard mixture over the pudding.

Stand the baking dish in a large roasting tin containing enough boiling water to come halfway up the sides of the dish. Bake in the oven for 30–40 minutes until the custard has set and the top is beginning to brown and crisp.

Melt the remaining jam in the same way and pour it over the top of the pudding, brushing as you go and making sure the whole berries are distributed evenly. Leave to stand for 10 minutes before serving.

VANILLA CASTER SUGAR

Keep a jar of unrefined caster sugar infused with used vanilla pods. Once the pods have served their purpose – either whole or split and scraped – to infuse custards etc., wash and dry, then submerge in a large jar of sugar to impart flavour and fragrance. There's no limit to the number of pods you can add!

APHRODITE'S PUDDING

We all know and love Eve's Pudding and it is perfectly obvious what fruits steam butterily and sugarily beneath its delectable sponge. However, the 'golden apple of the Hesperides', as quinces were known to the Greeks and Romans, was the apple that Paris gave to Aphrodite, the fruit of love, marriage and fertility. Put a quince on a mantelpiece and the room is scented with its almost narcissus-like scent. The fruit has a grainy texture like no other and an almost rusty colour if cut and not rubbed with lemon. The quince is fragrant and fresh, after pork, lamb or beef, but arm yourself, it does its best to resist peeling and coring.

serves 6

for the fruit layer

2 quinces
a spritz of lemon juice
30g butter, softened
2–3 tbsp vanilla caster sugar (see page 105)
3 strips of lemon peel
2 tbsp water
2 large Bramleys or other cooking apples

for the sponge

120g butter, softened
140g vanilla caster sugar (see page 105)
2 eggs
120g self-raising flour
finely grated zest of 1 lemon
1–2 tbsp milk (if needed)
1 tbsp demerara sugar (optional)

to serve

Jersey cream or pouring cream

Preheat the oven to 180°C/Gas 4. Peel, quarter and slice the quinces and toss in a little lemon juice to prevent discolouration.

Gently melt the butter in a large, heavy-bottomed frying pan, then throw in the quince slices, 2 tbsp vanilla sugar and the lemon peel. Cook for 15 minutes, stirring from time to time. Add the 2 tbsp water, cover with a lid and cook for a little longer, until the quince slices begin to soften.

Meanwhile, peel, core and thickly slice the apples. Add to the quinces and continue to cook gently until the apples begin to collapse. Taste and add a little more sugar if you need to, but I favour a sharp fruit mulch under a sweet sponge.

While the fruit is cooking, make the sponge. Using an electric mixer, or by hand, cream the butter with the sugar until pale and fluffy. Beat in the eggs, one at a time. Sift the flour over the mixture and fold in, together with the lemon zest. The mixture should have a 'dropping consistency' and plop off the spoon, but if it is a touch stiff, fold in a little milk, 1 tbsp at a time.

Turn the fruit into a baking dish and spoon the sponge mixture evenly on top. Bake for 40 minutes or so, sprinkling the demerara sugar over the sponge after 30 minutes for a crunchy top, if you like.

Serve with thick Jersey or pouring cream, your call.

STEAMED ORANGE SPONGE WITH SEVILLE ORANGE MARMALADE

For the first few weeks after I have made my Seville orange marmalade it retains the breath of the orange grove, the vibrant scent and flavour of the zesty oils, both lemon and orange, and the soft-set texture that plops from spoon to toast. Thereafter it firms up. It's the plopping and sharpness that work so well with a classic steamed sponge and even if you don't make your own marmalade, I'm sure you can find one that has the same effect. If you want a bit of fun, make some marmalade vodka (see below); my friends David and Izzy brought some to dinner before they knew they were going to be faced with the steaming marmalade pud. What a tandem.

serves 6

120g unsalted butter, softened
120g vanilla caster sugar (see page 105)
2 eggs
150g self-raising flour
1 tsp baking powder
⅓ tsp ground ginger
⅓ tsp ground allspice
finely grated zest of 1 lemon
a few drops of sweet orange oil (optional)
juice of ½ –1 orange
340g jar good bitter Seville orange marmalade
pouring cream, to serve

Cream the butter and sugar together until pale and fluffy, using an electric mixer or by hand. Beat in the eggs, one at a time, until evenly incorporated.

Sift the flour, baking powder and ground spices together over the mixture. Using a large metal spoon, fold in carefully, together with the lemon zest, orange oil, if using, and as much orange juice as you need to obtain a soft, dropping consistency.

Put the marmalade into the base of a greased 1.2 litre pudding basin and carefully spoon the sponge mixture on top. Cover the basin with a pleated sheet of greaseproof and pleated foil. Secure with string, tied tightly under the rim, leaving a length to act as a handle.

Put the basin in a large heavy-bottomed saucepan and pour in enough boiling water to come halfway up the side of the basin. Put the lid on, bring to the boil, then lower the heat and simmer for 2 hours, checking the water level from time to time and topping up with boiling water as necessary.

Lift the pudding basin out of the pan and remove the foil and greaseproof paper. Carefully run a palette knife around the edge of the pudding and then invert onto a warmed dish, deep enough to contain the sticky orange marmalade whooshing down the sides.

Serve with cream and shot glasses of marmalade vodka if you like.

MARMALADE VODKA

Put two-thirds of a jar of good-quality tawny marmalade (such as Oxford) in a sterilised kilner jar with 1 litre vodka. Seal and leave in a cool place for 2 weeks, turning it every so often. Strain and decant into little bottles for your friends, or simply your own delectation – with or without the pudding.

RHUBARB & STRAWBERRY CRISP WITH TOASTED OATS & HAZELNUTS

Crumbles and cobblers, crunches and crisps, what is it about the letter 'C' and its affinity with fruit, with puddings, with cream? Aren't we always trying to invent another comforter of a crumble, by rearranging the harmonies of butter, flour, sugar and the lesser notes of nut, oat, seed? After the early forced bright pink rhubarb grown in glasshouses, we wait until late spring or early summer for the outdoor fruit. It grows in thick clumps, the pure pink of the indoor now muddied with olive green, the stems stronger, broader, tougher, but just as delicious. Matching the acidity of rhubarb with strawberries creates one of those heavenly pairings that boasts the distinctiveness of each and the marriage of both.

serves 6

675g rhubarb, cleaned
4 tbsp vanilla caster sugar (see page 105)
450g strawberries, hulled, halved if large

for the crumble
large handful of jumbo oats
90g hazelnuts, toasted and skinned
180g plain flour
120g chilled butter, cut into cubes
60g light muscovado sugar
60g granulated sugar

to serve
pouring cream

Preheat the oven to 190°C/Gas 5. Cut the rhubarb into chunks and put into a large bowl. Sprinkle over the vanilla sugar and toss well, then add the strawberries and mix with your hands to get the juices to bleed together.

Heat a small frying pan over a medium-high heat, then sprinkle the jumbo oats into the pan and turn with a wooden spoon until crisped and biscuit brown. Tip onto a plate and set aside.

Grind two-thirds of the hazelnuts coarsely in a food processor, then tip in the flour, butter and sugars and pulse in brief spurts until amalgamated to a crumb texture.

Toss the fruit again and spoon into a baking dish. Scatter the crumble evenly on top. Sprinkle over the toasted oats. Coarsely chop the rest of the hazelnuts and sprinkle them over the top too.

Bake for 45 minutes or until browned and bubbling, the juices bursting through the crumb. Serve with cream.

RUM & BLACK CUSTARDS

Port and lemon, whisky Mac, gin and it, rum and black – rum and Ribena if you are feeling alliterative – they're not exactly the sophisticates of the cocktail universe, more the mainstays of the pub on the corner and the old lady having a 'medicinal' with her handbag on the table and her coat and hat still on. I served them in my first bar-maiding job and thought how grown-up they were. But back then I thought the height of sophistication was a Moscow Mule: vodka, lemonade, Angostura bitters and Roses lime cordial.

serves 4

300ml double cream (ideally Jersey)
finely grated zest of 1 lime
juice of 2 limes
1 tbsp light muscovado sugar
3 egg yolks
1 tbsp dark rum
1 tbsp crème de cassis (or myrtilles)
½ x 340g jar good blackcurrant jam, or 2 tbsp sharp blackcurrant purée

Preheat the oven to 170°C/Gas 3. In a large bowl, lightly whisk the cream with the lime zest, lime juice and sugar, just until evenly combined. Add the egg yolks and rum and whisk until amalgamated.

Stir the crème de cassis into the jam and spoon equally into 4 large ramekins or custard cups. Carefully pour the cream mixture over the jam.

Stand the ramekins in a roasting tin and pour in enough boiling water to come halfway up their sides. Lay a sheet of greaseproof paper over the top to prevent a skin forming on the custards.

Cook on the middle shelf of the oven for 30–35 minutes or until just set; if you gently shake the tin, the custards should tremble. Leave them to cool in the bain-marie where they will continue to cook in the residual heat.

Serve cool or warm.

RUM, RAISIN & MUSCOVADO ICE CREAM

There is something about February that leads me to heat. Be it musky spices, dusky sugar, tropical fruits or a sniff of dark rum. I want to see the light and pretend the buds are awaiting only a spring signal to break through. While I wait, I dream. I dream up a Caribbean ice cream with a nose of nutmeg scenting the raisins plumped in Jamaica rum. I add the toffee taste of muscovado sugar, a supple, sticky vanilla pod, Jersey cream. What a riff on the old vanilla ice cream and how well it works spooned onto a dark, caramelly papaya tatin (see page 132). Are you almost there?

serves 8–10

a handful of organic raisins
3 tbsp dark rum, or to taste
a grating of nutmeg
600ml whole milk (ideally Jersey)
1 vanilla pod, split, seeds scraped out
6 large egg yolks
120g light muscovado sugar
300ml Jersey or other rich double cream

Put the raisins into a small pan with 2 tbsp of the rum and heat gently to warm slightly. Remove from the heat, grate in a suspicion of nutmeg and leave the raisins to soak for an hour or two. They will have absorbed most of the liquor once fully plumped.

Slowly heat the milk in a heavy-bottomed pan with the scraped-out vanilla pod to scalding point. Meanwhile, in a large bowl, beat the egg yolks, muscovado sugar and vanilla seeds together thoroughly, then slowly pour on the hot milk, whisking as you do so. Pour back into the pan and whisk over a gentle heat until the mixture thickens enough to lightly coat the back of a spoon; don't let it boil or it will curdle. Pour the custard straight into a bowl set over ice, taking out the vanilla pod (to wash, dry and add to your vanilla caster sugar jar).

Whisk the cream in another bowl until it just holds its shape. When the custard is barely warm, fold in the cream and any liquor from the raisins. Taste. I usually add another 1 tbsp rum (no more), at this point. Too much alcohol can prevent an ice cream from setting and in any case you want to avoid an overwhelming taste of rum. You do, however, need to compensate for the diminishing effect of freezing on flavour.

Churn in an ice-cream maker until almost firm, then gently fold in the raisins. Transfer the pail to the freezer.

Remove the ice cream from the freezer 10–15 minutes before you want to serve it to soften slightly. Scoop into glasses or serve with baked bananas or atop my papaya tatin.

WHITE PEACHES IN MOSCATO WITH ZABAGLIONE ICE CREAM

One of the most memorable lunches I have ever eaten was at a café in the midst of the Asti vineyards at Valdivilla, above Santo Stefano Belbo in Piedmont. I remember white peaches drowning like wasps in nectar, the local nectar, Moscato d'Asti, the glut of warmth, the wine from across the road fizzing in the glass. Impossible to recreate as place and time and occasion are, the memory leads me, inexorably, to this recipe as in the nature of things, these occasions do.

serves 6

6 ripe white peaches
a spritz of lemon juice
1 tbsp vanilla caster sugar (see page 105), or to taste
1 bottle Moscato d'Asti spumante (if you can get it, if not, plain Moscato)

for the zabaglione ice cream (optional)
3 large egg yolks
90g vanilla caster sugar (see page 105)
150ml Moscato d'Asti
250ml double cream (ideally Jersey)

To make the ice cream, if serving, whisk the egg yolks, sugar and Moscato together in a large heatproof bowl, then place over a pan of simmering water, making sure the bowl is not touching the water. Carry on whisking (you are on a mission). The mixture will thicken, double in volume (at least) and turn light and frothy. Keep going. Eventually it will hold in a magical cloud. Remove the bowl from the pan and whisk for a few more minutes until cooled down. In another bowl, whip the cream to a ribbon consistency, then lightly fold into the whisked mixture.

Turn the mixture into a freezerproof tray, cover and freeze for an hour. Take the tray out of the freezer, scrape the hardening ice from the sides into the middle and return to the freezer. Repeat a couple of times until frozen. The texture is more like a parfait than an ice cream.

If you are going to skin the peaches, nick the skin and plunge them into a bowl of boiling hot water to cover for 30 seconds. Lift out, peel the peaches and roll them all over in a little lemon juice on a plate, then slice. Otherwise, slice them skin on, drop into a bowl and turn in a good spritz of lemon juice to prevent them discolouring. Sprinkle with the vanilla sugar and leave for a few minutes before turning gently with a spoon to amalgamate. Chill thoroughly.

Spoon the peaches into individual tall wine glasses and pour over the Moscato to cover. Serve the zabaglione ice cream, if you wish, atop the peaches or in bowls on the side. Heaven.

HOKEY POKEY WITH VANILLA ICE CREAM

Known as 'yellow man' in the North of Ireland, this gookily gorgeous childish treat is as fun to make as it is icky and sticky and licky to eat, a bit like the shards of honeycomb in a Crunchie bar. Try smashing it to smithereens and sprinkling it over home-made vanilla ice cream, or just eat it in chunks and chips. For children, it's instant fun and gratification. Once you add the bicarb it is like being back in the science labs at school as the whole pan begins to froth and the sugary liquid puffs up like a golden, bubbling cloud.

serves 8

for the vanilla ice cream
500ml whole milk (ideally Jersey)
2 vanilla pods, split, seeds scraped out
6 large egg yolks
140g vanilla caster sugar (see page 105)
600ml Jersey or other rich double cream

for the hokey pokey
60g light Muscovado sugar
2 tbsp golden syrup
1 tsp bicarbonate of soda

To make the ice cream, slowly heat the milk in a heavy-bottomed pan with the scraped-out vanilla pods to scalding point. Meanwhile, in a large bowl, beat the egg yolks, caster sugar and vanilla seeds together thoroughly, then slowly pour on the hot milk, whisking as you do so. Pour through a sieve back into the pan and whisk over a gentle heat until the mixture thickens enough to lightly coat the back of a spoon; don't let it boil or it is liable to curdle. Pour the custard straight into a bowl set over ice, taking out the vanilla pod (to wash, dry and add to your vanilla caster sugar jar).

When the custard has cooled to warm, fold in the cream. Churn in an ice-cream maker until thick and then finish freezing in the pail. The ice cream is best eaten within a day or two.

To make the hokey pokey, slowly melt the sugar and golden syrup together in a heavy-bottomed frying pan, stirring from time to time. Once the sugar has dissolved and the mixture is smooth, bring to a bubble and boil for 4 minutes, stirring every so often. Sprinkle the bicarbonate of soda over the mixture, stir to distribute evenly and cook for 30 seconds. Now tip the massed cloud of bubbling goo onto a baking tray lined with non-stick baking paper. Leave to cool and set.

About 10–15 minutes before serving, remove the ice cream from the freezer to allow it to soften slightly. Smash the hokey pokey into pieces. Scoop the ice cream into bowls and top with the hokey pokey.

Don't stir the hokey pokey into the ice cream before you churn it – it doesn't freeze, it turns to liquid caramel.

ELDERFLOWER SORBET

This sorbet is so scented and delicate and refreshing in June when you can pick the great white frothy heads of elder, the largest always out of reach, however tall you are. My daughter Charissa knocked them off the branches with a stick, when I sent her out to the hedges to pick for this recipe and for some cordial. Fill a trug or a basket – the flower-heads will shrink when steeped in sugar syrup, and you want maximum scenting. Serve with the amaretti (on page 124) or riciarelli (on page 125). (*Illustrated on previous page*)

serves 4–5

24–36 heads of elderflower
100g unrefined granulated sugar
250ml water
juice of 2–3 large lemons, to taste

Strip the elderflower heads from their stems using a fork and tie them in a piece of muslin. Set aside.

Put the sugar and water into a large, wide pan (one that will take the elderflowers later) and slowly bring to the boil, stirring occasionally to encourage the sugar to dissolve. Boil for 5 minutes to make a sugar syrup and remove from the heat.

Immerse the muslin bag of elderflowers in the hot sugar syrup, put the lid on and leave to cool completely.

Remove the muslin and squeeze with every ounce of your might, to extract as much scented liquid as possible. Gradually add the lemon juice, tasting as you do so. A sorbet will taste sweeter once frozen, so the tart side of sweet is infinitely preferable.

Churn the syrup in an ice-cream maker until firm. If you do not have one, freeze in a sealed suitable container, remembering to beat the freezing mixture from the sides of the container into the middle every hour to break down the ice crystals.

Once frozen, either eat straight away or keep in a sealed container in the freezer, taking it out about 10 minutes before serving to soften slightly. The flavour diminishes quite quickly, so eat within a week.

Scoop into glasses and accompany with little dessert biscuits.

PASSION FRUIT, COCONUT & LIME SORBET

Something heady and light and redolent of the tropics after the substance of a handsomely hefty winter dinner. You may make your own amaretti or ricciarelli to go with this ice if you feel so moved, which, when you try the recipes (on pages 124 and 125 respectively), might be rather more often than you would think.

serves 6–8

120g unrefined granulated sugar
600ml water
9 ripe passion fruit (ripe when wrinkly, curiously)
finely grated zest and juice of 2 limes
½ x 400ml tin organic coconut cream

Put the sugar and water into a wide-based pan and bring slowly to the boil, stirring occasionally until the sugar has dissolved. Boil for 5 minutes to make your sugar syrup. Leave to cool slowly, or pour into a bowl set over a larger bowl of ice cubes to speed it up.

Halve the passion fruit, extract 2 tsp of the seeds and set aside. Scoop out the rest of the passion fruit flesh into a sieve set over a bowl. Press with the back of a wooden spoon to extract as much juice as you can. Tip the remaining pulp from the sieve into a small pan and warm gently, then press in the sieve again.

Stir the passion fruit juice and lime juice into the cooled sugar syrup along with the coconut cream.

Churn the mixture in an ice-cream maker until slushy and then add the lime zest and reserved passion fruit seeds. Continue to churn until the sorbet is firm. (Alternatively, freeze the sorbet in a covered freezerproof tray, whisking the mixture every hour until set to a slushy texture, then stir in the lime zest and passion fruit seeds.) Freeze until properly set with no crystals.

Either serve the sorbet straight away or keep it in a sealed container in the freezer, taking it out about 10 minutes before serving to soften slightly. For optimum flavour, eat within a week.

POMEGRANATE SORBET

I served this intensely flavoured crimson jewel of a sorbet with the lemon and coconut cream tart (on page 133) and the flavours and colour-clash worked brilliantly. If you are serving it on its own there will be enough for 4, but it would be good accompanied by another fruit sorbet or ice cream and home-made amaretti (see page 124).

serves 4–5

5 pomegranates
100g unrefined granulated sugar
250ml water
a spritz of lemon or lime juice

Halve the pomegranates, scoop out 1 tbsp of the seeds, avoiding the bitter membrane, and set aside.

Squeeze the juice from the pomegranate halves, using a citrus squeezer. It works well, if a little messily, and you can press any pulped seed remaining in the squeezer with your fingers to extract the maximum amount of juice, before discarding and carrying on with the next pomegranate. You should get around 250ml juice. Set aside.

Make the sugar syrup by dissolving the sugar in the water in a pan over a medium heat, stirring occasionally, and then boiling for 5 minutes. Leave to cool or pour into a bowl set over a larger bowl of ice to hasten the cooling.

Pour the pomegranate juice into the sugar syrup, stir and add a small squeeze of lemon or lime. Taste. You need just enough citrus juice to sharpen and bring out the flavour of the pomegranate.

Churn the syrup in an ice-cream maker until firm. (Or freeze in a sealed suitable container, beating the freezing mixture from the sides into the middle every hour to break down the ice crystals.) Either serve straight away or keep in a sealed container in the freezer, taking it out about 10 minutes before serving to soften slightly. As with all fruit sorbets, the flavour diminishes quite quickly, so eat within a week.

Scoop into glass dishes and scatter the reserved pomegranate seeds on top. Accompany with amaretti or other dessert biscuits.

ELLIE'S AMARETTI

Murray's deli in Clevedon, Somerset, is my Aladdin's Cave. Three generations of the Italian Murray family have kept this gem near the Victorian beauty of Clevedon pier going. Ellie Murray makes these stunning amaretti, Miranda the riciarelli. But there is no competition, both are the best of their kind. Start the amaretti off the night before you wish to eat them, you will see why below. (*Illustrated on previous page*)

makes 20 or so

200g blanched Marcona almonds (ideally), or ready-ground almonds
200g vanilla caster sugar (see page 105)
1 tsp natural almond extract
3–4 egg whites
unrefined icing sugar, to sprinkle

Line two baking sheets with non-stick baking paper. If you've bought whole almonds, grind them in a blender or food processor.

In a large bowl, mix the ground almonds and caster sugar together and stir in the almond extract. Gradually stir in the egg whites (don't beat them first). The texture should be like wet sand – quite firm and not too sticky.

Roll the mixture into small balls, each about the size of a walnut, and place a few centimetres apart on the baking sheets. Flatten the tops slightly with your thumb. Sift icing sugar generously over the tops and leave in a cool place overnight, to ensure they will hold their shape and have the characteristic cracked appearance after baking.

Preheat the oven to 170°C/Gas 3. Bake the amaretti for 20–25 minutes or until pale golden brown. Transfer the baking sheet to a wire rack and leave for a few minutes to allow the amaretti to firm up slightly before flipping them onto the rack to cool.

PISTACHIO AMARETTI

Prepare the amaretti mixture and roll into balls as above. Grind 120g pistachios in a food processor until finely chopped, scatter on a board and roll the amaretti in the chopped pistachios. Bake as above.

CITRUS AMARETTI

Add the finely grated zest of 2 lemons and 2 oranges to the ground almonds with the sugar. Replace one of the egg whites with 1 tbsp lemon juice and 1 tbsp orange juice.

RICIARELLI

These almondy biscuits are a lovely accompaniment to a fruit ice cream or sorbet; their almond crumb defines the word deliquesce.

makes 10–12

180g blanched Marcona almonds (ideally), or ready-ground almonds
2 medium egg whites
15g plain flour
⅓ tsp baking powder
120g unrefined icing sugar, plus extra to dust
a few drops of natural almond extract

Preheat the oven to 220°C/Gas 7. Line a large baking sheet with non-stick baking paper. If you've bought whole almonds, grind them in a blender or food processor.

Whisk the egg whites in a clean, dry bowl until stiff. Sift the flour and baking powder together over the egg whites and then fold in, using a large metal spoon or spatula. Sift the icing sugar over the mixture and fold in. Finally incorporate the ground almonds and almond extract to make a soft paste.

Dust your work surface generously with icing sugar. Take a heaped dessertspoonful of the mixture, roll in the icing sugar and form into an oblong, using the palm of your hand. Place on the prepared baking sheet. Repeat to shape the rest of the mixture, spacing the oblongs well apart.

Bake for 10–12 minutes or until the biscuits are golden and slightly cracked on the surface, yet still soft inside. Place the baking sheet on a wire rack and leave for a few minutes, then transfer the ricarelli to the rack and leave to cool.

A FEW SWEET TARTS...

There is no limit to the tart, apart from not over-zealously throwing everything at it and crowding it out. Over-stuffed and over-laden with a cornucopia is not the point. A couple, or maybe three dominant ingredients are all you need, for the real pleasure lies, as we all know, in depth of flavour and in the collation of twin textures: perfectly crisp, slim, butter-crust with silken creamy filling and fruit; or sharp, caramel-bitter fruit dazzling on its own. Or the goo of cakey crumb enhanced with almond, hazelnut, walnut or treacle. Or plain chocolate, as plain and dark and fruity a chocolate as gives complexity, with little else to help it bar coffee, vanilla, almond, butter, cream.

Difficult to beat an almondy Bakewell or a classic tarte au citron – made with more eggs than is generally considered sane, and enough cream, vanilla sugar, zest and juice to set to a quakey gel. All proportions are, or should be, highly personalised. I prefer the lemon to verge on extreme taste-bud assault before settling down into acquiescence at its daring sharpness. On the other hand, a Bakewell lulls you into sweet security but needs an almost-too-much edge of bitter almond to offset the jam and sugar.

I really can't think of a lunch or dinner where a sweet tart or tatin isn't utterly irresistible, unless you've just eaten a savoury tart or pie.

PEAR & BLUEBERRY TATIN

Williams pears have their very own, very particular taste, texture – neither the graininess of a Conference nor the liquid pulp of a Comice – and they hold great depth of flavour when cooked. But please use a pear of your choice when William isn't to be found. This is a joyous tart, lavishly purple, turning prose to poetry, with such a fine crust that it crisps, but doesn't sog under the weight of the berries. Yes, they produce a lot of juice but I spoon it over each slice and use very little sugar – only what's necessary for the caramelisation. (*Also illustrated on previous page*)

serves 6

for the pastry
120g plain flour
60g chilled unsalted butter, cut into cubes
1 tbsp ice-cold water

for the filling
3 pears (ideally Williams)
spritz of lemon juice
90g unrefined caster sugar
knob of butter (the size of a walnut), cut into small pieces
300g blueberries

to serve
Jersey or other rich double cream

To make the pastry, sift the flour into a food processor, add the butter cubes and pulse briefly to a crumb texture. Add the chilled water through the feeder tube and pulse until the dough coheres into a ball, adding a little more water if necessary. Wrap the pastry in cling film, flatten slightly with the palm of your hand and chill in the fridge for 30 minutes.

Meanwhile, for the filling, peel, halve and core the pears and rub the cut surfaces with a little lemon juice to prevent discolouration. Pour the sugar into a 23cm tatin tin (or heavy-bottomed ovenproof frying pan) and shake to spread evenly. Place over a low heat and watch like a hawk as the sugar melts, dissolves, turns pale biscuit in colour, then to a mahogany caramel, but do not stir – just shake the pan if the sugar is melting unevenly. At the point at which it begins to bubble, remove from the heat and add the little knobs of butter. Arrange the pear halves, cut side down, in the syrup, radiating out from the middle with one in the centre. Fill the gaps in between with blueberries. Leave to cool.

Preheat the oven to 190°C/Gas 5. Roll out the pastry on a lightly floured surface to a round, a little larger than the diameter of your pan. Lift the pastry on the rolling pin and drape it over the fruit in the pan. Tuck the edges down the sides of the pan to seal in the fruit. Bake for 40 minutes or until the pastry is biscuit coloured and you can see purple juices breaking through at the edges.

Leave for 10 minutes before inverting onto a large plate (deep enough to contain the juices) and carefully removing the tin. Serve with thick cream.

PAPAYA TATIN

I chanced upon the papaya relatively recently as a scented fleshed fruit whose caviar-like seeds had to be scooped out like so many beads before you could attempt the apricot coloured flesh within. A little bit under-ripe and the fruit has a lethal bitterness, a little too ripe and it turns cotton-wooly.

When I checked the papaya out in Jane Grigson's seminal *Fruit Book*, wondering whether it collapsed during cooking, or, indeed, whether you could cook it at all, I found recipes for stuffed papaya, ginger-baked papaya, Hawaiian papaya chowder and papaya upside-down cake. Little did I know, clearly.

Here is my take on the papaya, a dark caramel syrupy tatin, the fruit holding its shape perfectly. Served with a scoop of the rum, raisin and muscovado ice cream (on page 111) the pathway to heaven is short and clear.

serves 6

for the pastry
200g packet all-butter ready made puff pastry or shortcrust made with 180g plain flour, 90g chilled unsalted butter and 1–2 tbsp cold water

for the filling
3 papayas
juice of ½ lime
90g vanilla caster sugar (see page 105)
60g unsalted butter, cut into small pieces

to serve
Jersey or other rich double cream, or ice cream

If making your own shortcrust pastry, follow the method on page 131 and chill for 30 minutes.

Meanwhile, for the filling, halve the papayas, scoop out the seeds and peel away the skin. Sprinkle the cut surfaces with the lime juice. Pour the sugar into a 23cm tatin tin (or heavy-bottomed ovenproof frying pan) and shake to spread evenly. Place over a low heat and keep a close eye on the pan as the sugar liquefies, turns golden, then to a mahogany-coloured caramel, but do not stir. If it appears to be melting unevenly, shake the pan to re-distribute. The moment it begins to bubble, remove from the heat and add the little knobs of butter. The mixture will fizzle and caramelise, turning dark and sticky.

Immediately press the papaya halves, cut side up, into the sticky caramel, radiating from the centre like the spokes of a wheel. If the fruit won't quite fit, trim the slim ends and use the pieces to fill the gaps. Leave to cool.

Preheat the oven to 190°C/Gas 5. Roll out the pastry on a lightly floured surface to a round, a little larger than the diameter of your pan. Lift the pastry on the rolling pin and drape it over the fruit in the pan. Tuck the edges down the sides of the pan to seal in the fruit like a blanket. Bake for about 40 minutes or until the pastry is golden and dark goo is bubbling at the edges. Place the tin on a rack and leave for 10 minutes before inverting onto a large lipped plate (deep enough to hold the caramelised juices).

Serve warm, with cream or ice cream.

LEMON & COCONUT CREAM TART

In the canon of sweet tarts there are a few classics that hit the roof, the stratosphere, that make temples of the word tart. Above them all – and this is entirely subjective – are tartes au citron and tatin, treacle and della nonna, chocolate, and apple. I tinker a little each time I make them, but I wouldn't meddle with a classic. There is, after all, a certain expectation if you say the words 'tarte au citron'. I have kept this lemon and coconut tart citrus-sharp and injected that note of Far Eastern exoticism to the gelled softness of the lemon custard.

Oh my, will I do it again? Yes, I will. All takers were asked to detect the new note in the scale of happiness and harmony and, second or third bites in, caught a wave of it. Lemon and coconut is desert-island good.

serves 6

for the pastry

180g plain flour
120g chilled unsalted butter, cut into cubes
50g unrefined icing sugar
1 egg yolk, beaten
1 tbsp ice-cold water, plus a little extra if needed
a little egg white, for brushing

for the filling

6 large eggs
250g vanilla caster sugar (see page 105)
200ml double cream (ideally Jersey)
200ml coconut milk
finely grated zest of 2 large Sicilian or 3 ordinary lemons
juice of 3 large Sicilian lemons or 4 ordinary lemons (or more to taste)

To make the pastry, sift the flour into a food processor, add the butter and sift in the icing sugar. Pulse briefly until the mixture resembles crumbs, then add the egg yolk and chilled water through the feeder tube and pulse until the dough coheres into a ball, adding a little more water if necessary. Wrap the pastry in cling film, flatten slightly with the palm of your hand and chill in the fridge for 30 minutes.

Meanwhile make the filling. Whisk the eggs and sugar together in a large bowl, then whisk in the cream, coconut milk, lemon zest and most of the lemon juice, until evenly combined. Taste and add more lemon juice if you wish – it depends how tart you like your tart. Pour the filling into a jug.

Preheat the oven to 180°C/Gas 4. Lightly grease a 26cm tart tin. Roll out the pastry on a lightly floured surface and use to line the prepared tin, leaving the excess overhanging the rim. Prick the base with a fork. Line the pastry case with a sheet of baking parchment and a layer of baking beans. Bake 'blind' in the oven for 15 minutes, then remove the paper and beans and return to the oven for 5 minutes to dry the base.

Take out the pastry case and trim off the excess pastry. Lower the oven setting to 150°C/Gas 2. Quickly and lightly brush the inside of the pastry case with a little egg white to seal and pour in the custard. Bake for 35–45 minutes or until the custard is just set, but with a slight tremble when you shake the tin. (It will continue to firm up slightly on cooling.) Remove from the oven and place on a wire rack to cool.

Serve still slightly warm, without cream.

NOTE

You may make this tart a few hours before you want to cut it, but it needs to be eaten on the day it is made.

TORTA DELLA NONNA

I do not wish to appear to be culturally appropriating either a tart or a grandmother I don't actually own, as it were, but the notion of the Italian grandmother will suffice to get you in the mood for a tart that is, at once, all about tradition; and whilst being a cheap tart – these are all ingredients that any self-respecting home cook will have to hand – it is nonetheless, as worthy as our Bakewell, treacle or lemon meringue. It is one of those national dishes of which, it is said, there are as many recipes as there are, well, in this case, grandmothers, mothers, maiden-aunts, lovers, bambini. No, it is not difficult; it is simply more-ish with its lemon-peel scented custard, toasted pine nuts and bitter chocolate.

serves 8

for the pastry
180g plain flour
1 heaped tbsp unrefined icing sugar
90g chilled unsalted butter, cut into cubes
grated zest of 1 lemon
1 egg yolk, beaten
2–3 tsp ice-cold water
a little egg white, for brushing

for the filling
500ml whole milk (ideally Jersey)
finely pared zest of 1 lemon, in 3–4 strips (pared with a potato peeler and any white pith removed)
1 vanilla pod, split, seeds scraped out
90g unrefined granulated sugar
4 large egg yolks
2 tbsp cornflour
knob of butter (the size of a walnut)

to finish
90g pine nuts, toasted in a dry pan
30–45g piece of dark chocolate (about 70% cocoa solids), for grating

To make the pastry, sift the flour and icing sugar into a food processor, add the butter cubes and pulse briefly until the mixture resembles crumbs. Add the lemon zest, egg yolk and 2 tsp chilled water through the feeder tube and pulse until the dough coheres into a ball, adding a little more water if necessary.

Wrap the pastry in cling film, flatten slightly with the palm of your hand and chill in the fridge for 30 minutes.

Preheat the oven to 180°C/Gas 4. Lightly grease a 23cm tart tin. Roll out the pastry on a lightly floured surface and use to line the prepared tin, leaving the excess overhanging the rim. Line the pastry case with a sheet of baking parchment and a layer of baking beans. Bake 'blind' in the oven for 20 minutes. Trim off the excess pastry.

Remove the paper and beans from the pastry case. Prick the base and sides with a fork and bake for a further 7–10 minutes or until cooked, pale biscuit-coloured and crisp. Quickly and lightly brush with a little egg white to seal and keep crisp. Transfer to a wire rack.

While the pastry case is baking, make the tart filling. In a heavy-bottomed pan over a low heat, warm the milk with the lemon zest, vanilla pod and seeds, and half of the sugar. Meanwhile, whisk the egg yolks and remaining sugar together in a large bowl, then whisk in the cornflour. Pour in a little of the hot milk, whisking as you do so to keep the mixture smooth, then slowly whisk in the remaining hot milk. Pour back into the pan and whisk over the heat until thickened; this will only take a couple of minutes. Remove the lemon zest and vanilla pod. Pour the custard back into the bowl and whisk in the butter. Cool to warm.

Spoon the custard into the warm tart case and leave to cool, then chill in the fridge for an hour or so until ready to serve.

Scatter the toasted pine nuts over the surface of the tart and grate a storm of dark chocolate on top before serving.

GÂTEAU BASQUE

Sugar-crisp frangipane top contrasting with sweet, set-firm vanilla custard is a joy, a real top-class pud to serve at smart-tart dinners, more casual suppers or lunch in the garden. The pâtissiers of Toulouse, with their proximity to the Pyrenees and the Spanish border, are rife with variations of this lovely Basque cake-cum-tart. Do not be deterred by the two stages; think of simply having less to do the day you cook. Frangipane is stickier to roll out than normal pastry, so you will need a very well-floured rolling pin. If it breaks, just patch and press it into the tin.

Eat warm with a few berries tossed in kirsch and sugar, on its own, or with a hit of espresso. As good the next morning with coffee, still crisp with gushing custard.

serves 8

for the frangipane pastry
250g butter, softened
450g vanilla caster sugar (see page 105)
1 whole egg, plus 3 extra yolks
finely grated zest of 1 lemon
a few drops of natural almond extract
320g plain flour
1 tbsp baking powder
½ tsp salt
100g blanched Marcona almonds (ideally), freshly ground, or good ready-ground almonds
1 egg yolk, beaten with 1 tsp milk, to glaze

for the crème patissière
600ml whole milk
1 vanilla pod, split, seeds scraped out
1 whole egg, plus 6 extra yolks
120g vanilla caster sugar (see page 105)
45g cornflour
15g plain flour

To make the frangipane pastry, put the softened butter and vanilla sugar into a food mixer and beat until light and fluffy. Add the whole egg and beat until incorporated, then add the 3 egg yolks, lemon zest and almond extract and beat until evenly combined. Sift half of the flour with the baking powder over the mixture and beat to combine, then repeat with the rest of the flour and the salt. Now add the ground almonds and fold in, using a spatula or large metal spoon.

Tip the mixture out onto a piece of cling film, wrap and flatten a little with the palm of your hand. Refrigerate overnight.

To make the crème patissière, slowly heat the milk in a heavy-based pan with the empty vanilla pod to scalding point. Meanwhile, in a large bowl, beat the whole egg, egg yolks, sugar and vanilla seeds together, then beat in the cornflour and flour until smooth. Slowly pour on the hot milk, whisking as you do so. Pour through a sieve back into the pan and whisk over a gentle heat for 4–5 minutes until the mixture thickens considerably, keeping it smooth. Pour the crème patissière straight into a bowl set over ice to cool it quickly.

Meanwhile, lightly grease a 20cm tart tin. Preheat the oven to 180°C/Gas 4 with a baking sheet inside to heat up. Unwrap the frangipane and divide in two, one piece slightly larger than the other. Roll out the larger piece on a floured surface to a round and use to line the tart tin, pressing the pastry in and patching as necessary. Spread the crème patissière evenly in the pastry case, using a spatula (it won't matter if the filling is still a little warm).

Roll out the other piece of pastry to make a lid and position over the filling. Trim off the excess pastry, then use a fork to crimp and seal the pastry edges together. With a sharp knife tip, lightly score a pattern of curved rays, Pithiviers-style, from the centre to the edge. Brush the egg glaze over the surface. Bake on the hot baking sheet for 50 minutes or until the top is browned and crisped. Transfer to a wire rack and cool to warm or cold before serving.

MIRANDA'S LUSCIOUS LEMON CAKE

Miranda, daughter no. 1, has been my right-hand girl on *Irresistible*, helping me cook-the-book for the photographs with her characteristic élan. This is her story about a very special cake: 'I have always been jealous of my mum's Kitchen Aid and this year she generously gave me one as a Christmas present. In true rebellious style I decided to christen it with the kind of cake that we were never allowed to eat when we were little. Icing sugar was banned, butter icing was off the list, white flour was not welcome in our house. I always promised myself I would make huge, rich, butter-iced, white-floured skyscraper cakes when I grew up. I wanted this cake to bedazzle, to have everything, to be so irresistible that even my mum would hack off a chunk and devour it. So, giggling to myself, I baked a lemon sponge, made butter icing, lemon syrup and frosting, crystallised some rose petals in sugar… I really went for it.'

makes a deep 20cm cake

450g unsalted butter, softened
450g vanilla caster sugar (see page 105)
8 eggs
450g self-raising flour
finely grated zest of 3 lemons
juice of 1–2 lemons

for the lemon butter icing
140g unsalted butter, softened
280g icing sugar
finely grated zest of 1 lemon
1 tbsp lemon juice

for the lemon drizzle
juice of 1½ lemons
85g unrefined caster sugar

for the lemon frosting
175g icing sugar
1 tbsp lemon juice

to finish
1 small fragrant pink rose
1 egg white, lightly beaten
caster sugar, for coating
1 lemon, for zesting

Preheat the oven to 180°C/Gas 4. Grease and line two 20cm springform cake tins. Cream the butter and sugar together in a food mixer (or by hand) until light and fluffy, then beat in the eggs, one at a time. Sift the flour over the mixture, then fold it in gently with a metal spoon, together with the lemon zest, adding as much of the lemon juice as you need to give a soft, dropping consistency.

Divide the mixture between the prepared tins, spreading it evenly, and bake on the middle shelf of the oven for 40 minutes, or until a skewer inserted into the centre comes out clean; the cakes may need an extra 10 minutes or so. Stand the tins on wire racks for 20 minutes, before turning the sponges out onto the racks to cool completely.

To make the butter icing, beat all the ingredients together in a bowl until smooth, light and fluffy. Lay the first sponge on a large plate and spread the butter icing evenly on top, then place the other sponge on top.

For the lemon drizzle, gently heat the lemon juice and caster sugar together in a small pan to dissolve the sugar and then boil for 5 minutes. Skewer holes over the surface of the top sponge and slowly pour the warm lemon drizzle syrup evenly over.

To make the frosting, whisk the icing sugar and lemon juice together in a bowl, then pour on top of the cake to cover, allowing it to run ragged down the sides. Put the cake in the fridge until the frosting has set to a translucent white.

Meanwhile, for a little extra touch, crystallise some rose petals. Pull the petals off the rose. One at a time, paint the petals with egg white and then dip into the caster sugar to coat all over. Shake off the excess and then lay on a sheet of non-stick baking paper to dry (a warm kitchen will hasten drying). The petals are ready when they feel crisp rather than limp.

Just before serving, zest a lemon over the frosting and arrange the crystallised rose petals on top.

CARAWAY SEED & LEMON CAKE

There is something hideously Victorian, prudish, un-epicurean sounding about a seed cake that has prevented me from making one for all these years. Then I stumbled upon the idea of flavouring it with the zest of a Sicilian lemon. Any good, unwaxed lemon will do, but please do not be tempted to add more caraway seeds, or you will introduce a medicinal, musty taste. If you use eggs like Burford browns with their sunshine yolks, the cake will turn out a brilliant canary yellow.

A glass of Madeira and a slice of this mid-morning might have been the Victorian solution to hunger pangs, but I served it after lunch with glasses of 20-year-old Pedro Ximénez sherry, as sticky brown sweet as any linctus. I served blueberries doused in crème de myrtilles on the side, but crème de cassis would do. Epicurean in full measure.

makes a 900g loaf cake

120g butter, softened
120g vanilla caster sugar (see page 105)
3 large eggs
1 heaped tsp caraway seeds
grated zest of 1 large lemon (ideally Sicilian)
170g self-raising flour
60g ground almonds
2 tbsp milk

Preheat the oven to 170°C/Gas 3 and put a baking sheet inside to heat up. Line a 23 x 12cm loaf tin with non-stick baking paper.

Cream the butter and sugar together in a food mixer (or by hand) until light and fluffy. Beat in the eggs, one at a time, then add the caraway seeds and lemon zest. Sift the flour over the mixture and fold in, together with the ground almonds. Finally fold in the milk.

Scrape the mixture into the prepared loaf tin, spread evenly and place the tin on the heated baking sheet. Bake for about 1 hour until lightly browned on top, but test with a skewer after 50 minutes – insert into the middle and it should emerge clean.

Leave the cake to cool in the tin on a wire rack for 10 minutes, then turn out onto the rack and leave to cool completely.

HONEY SPICE CAKE WITH GINGER & COCONUT

Light and damp and spicy, the fresh ginger juice and spice and coconut make this loaf cake irresistible at any time of day: I adopted it from a recipe of Dan Lepard's, one of my favourite bakers.

makes a 900g loaf cake

3cm thumb of fresh root ginger (unpeeled)
2 tbsp strong-flavoured runny honey (such as chestnut)
2 tsp golden syrup
150g unsalted butter, softened
60g dark muscovado sugar
2 eggs
150g self-raising flour
1 tsp baking powder
1 tsp ground cinnamon
1 tsp freshly ground allspice
1 generous tbsp organic coconut milk (thick, creamy milk from the top)

Preheat the oven to 170°C/Gas 3. Line a 23 x 12cm loaf tin with non-stick baking paper.

Grate the root ginger, skin on, onto a small piece of muslin, then draw the edges together and squeeze tightly over a bowl until the ginger has exuded all its juice and all that remains in the muslin is dry residue to chuck away.

Warm the honey, golden syrup, butter and brown sugar together gently in a small pan until the butter has melted. Transfer to an electric mixer bowl and beat for a couple of minutes, then add the eggs and ginger juice and continue to beat for a further 2 minutes to aerate and lighten the mixture.

Sift the flour, baking powder and spices over the mixture, then fold in, together with the thick coconut milk, until evenly combined.

Scrape the mixture into the prepared loaf tin and bake for 40–50 minutes or until a skewer inserted into the middle comes out clean. You should check at 40 minutes, but I find this cake often takes 50 minutes.

Stand the tin on a wire rack for 30 minutes, then turn the cake out onto the rack and cool to barely warm to eat.

SUMMER BERRY GÉNOISE

This is a little slice of summer decadence. It looks like the spirit of summer and it tastes like it too. You may serve simply the strained cream and berries if the sponge is a layer too far for you. However, the impact of the high-piled hyperbole is worth it, and there is no cream involved nor butter in the sponge; it is all airy-fairy lightness if you are searching for excuses. Remember to allow an hour to strain the fromage frais, mascarpone and yoghurt of their watery, lactic juices.

serves 8

for the cream
250g mascarpone
150g good-quality fromage frais (ideally La Faissette)
2 heaped tbsp live thick Greek-style yoghurt
1 vanilla pod, split, seeds scraped out
finely grated zest of 1 lemon
2 tbsp light muscovado sugar, or to taste
1 egg white

for the génoise sponge
4 large eggs
100g vanilla caster sugar (see page 105)
100g self-raising flour

for the berry mound
675g summer fruits in season, such as strawberries, raspberries, blueberries, stoned cherries, redcurrants and blackcurrants
2 heaped tbsp redcurrant jelly

For the génoise, preheat the oven to 180°C/Gas 4 and butter a 20cm cake tin.

For the cream, place a muslin-lined large sieve over a bowl and scrape the mascarpone, fromage frais and yoghurt into it. Leave to drain for an hour, or longer (up to 2 hours) if it suits you better.

Meanwhile, make the génoise. Put the eggs and sugar into a large bowl set over a pan of barely simmering water and whisk until the mixture is pale and light, and thick enough to leave a trail on the surface when you lift the beaters up. Remove the bowl from the pan. Sift the flour over the surface of the mixture, then fold it in deeply but gently until fully amalgamated.

Spoon the mixture into the prepared tin and bake for 20 minutes or until golden and springy to the touch. Leave in the tin on a wire rack for 10 minutes, then turn the sponge out onto the rack and let it cool completely.

To finish the cream, pull up all four corners of the muslin and squeeze out the remaining liquid. Pour the liquid away, then turn the contents of the muslin out into the sieve. Push them through into the empty bowl, with a wooden spoon. Fold in the vanilla seeds, lemon zest and sugar to taste. Whisk the egg white in a separate bowl to firm peaks and lightly fold into the cream.

Place the génoise on a large plate and cover with the cream, then pile the berries on top. Melt the redcurrant jelly with a tiny splash of water and stir until smooth. Brush the redcurrant glaze over the berries until they glisten.

PASSION FRUIT DRIZZLE CAKE

I was determined to make my neighbour Patricia a special birthday cake she wouldn't have come across before. After all, by the time you're thirty plus V.A.T., you've gone around the chocolate block a few times and are probably more worried about eating your cake than having it. A twist on a lemon drizzle, I thought. Perhaps passion fruit – sharp, intense, pulpy, seedy, brilliant yellow – yep, that seemed to be the one. As far as the celebrants were concerned, it was clearly the business. The cake seemed to melt away. I made it again with freshly ground Marcona almonds replacing half the flour. The gooey almondy sponge worked brilliantly with the passion fruit twang. I'm going to claim it as my newest classic, it's that good.

makes a 900g loaf cake

170g butter, softened
85g light muscovado caster sugar
85g unrefined caster sugar
2 large eggs
grated zest of 2 lemons
170g self-raising flour (I used half wholemeal/half white, but do as you please)
1 tsp baking powder
pinch of sea salt
3–5 tbsp milk

for the passion fruit drizzle
5 large passion fruit
1½ –2 tsp caster or demerara sugar, to taste

Preheat the oven to 180°C/Gas 4. Butter a 900g loaf tin and line the base with buttered non-stick baking paper.

Cream the butter and both sugars together, using an electric mixer, until light and fluffy. Now beat in the eggs, one at a time, using a wooden spoon. Throw in the lemon zest, then sift the flour, baking powder and salt over the mixture. Fold together gently, using a spatula or large metal spoon, adding 3 tbsp milk as you do so. Add more of the milk if necessary, to achieve a soft, dropping consistency.

Scrape the mixture into the prepared tin and lightly smooth the top. Bake on the middle shelf of the oven, until golden and well risen. Check after 40 minutes by inserting a skewer into the middle; it should emerge clean. The cake might need an extra 5–10 minutes, but always check early. Place the loaf tin on a wire rack and leave to cool for 20 minutes.

Meanwhile, for the drizzle, halve the passion fruit and reserve a heaped teaspoonful of the seeds. Scoop the rest of the pulp and seeds into a sieve over a small pan and press to extract as much juice as possible. Add the sugar to the pan, dissolve over a medium heat and then let bubble to reduce until syrupy, about 2 minutes. Taste. It should be sharp, so only add more sugar if it really needs it.

Turn the cake out and place the right way up on the rack. While still warmth, spike the sponge deeply with a skewer all over, from the top almost to the bottom. Immediately pour the passion fruit syrup evenly over the surface – it will dribble into the holes and down the sides of the cake. Scatter the reserved passion fruit seeds over the top.

Eat warm, with or without yoghurt or crème fraîche.

CHOCOLATE STRAWBERRY JAM CAKE

There is something gloriously nursery tea-ish about the idea of combining strawberry – or raspberry – jam with chocolate. It's so politically incorrect in the world of puritan, plain chocolate worshippers, who would put neither fruit nor spice near solid cocoa. Here the deep indentation glossed with pip and jam and red against black, the very sweetness offsetting the bitter dark, is the apogee of pleasure. Even the child who prefers milk to plain will be seduced by its magic.

makes a 20cm cake

90g blanched Marcona almonds
150g dark chocolate (64–72% cocoa solids)
2 tbsp espresso-strength hot coffee
90g unsalted butter, cut into cubes
90g vanilla caster sugar (see page 105)
3 large eggs, separated
1 level tbsp plain flour
170g (½ jar) good strawberry or raspberry jam (I use Wilkin & Sons Tiptree)

Preheat the oven to 170°C/Gas 3 and put a baking sheet inside to heat up. Butter a 20cm loose-bottomed cake tin generously. Grind the almonds in a food processor until almost fine.

Break up the chocolate and put it into a heatproof bowl with the coffee. Melt over a pan of barely simmering water, making sure the bowl is not touching the water.

Add the butter, sugar and ground almonds to the melted chocolate and then remove the pan from the heat, keeping the bowl in place over the hot water. Stir the mixture until it is well amalgamated. Add the egg yolks, one at a time, stirring them in quickly and thoroughly.

In a large clean bowl, whisk the egg whites until they hold fairly stiff peaks.

Scrape the chocolate mixture into another large bowl and stir in 1 tbsp of the whisked egg white to loosen the mixture. Sift the flour lightly over the mixture and fold it in, using a large metal spoon. Now lightly but thoroughly fold in the rest of the whisked egg whites, a spoonful at a time. Spoon the mixture into the prepared tin and gently level the surface.

In a small pan over a low heat, warm the jam very slightly. Now drop the jam in spoonfuls onto the surface of the cake mixture and work it down into the mixture with a skewer.

Bake for 40–50 minutes or until a skewer inserted into the centre comes out clean. Test first at 40 minutes, but expect the cake to take nearer to 50 minutes.

Leave to cool in the tin on a rack for 20 minutes or so, then push the base of the tin up to release it from the sides. Leave the cake to cool on its base on the rack.

Best eaten slightly warm with cold clotted cream or crème fraîche.

CHOCOLATE & MORELLO CHERRY FRIDGE CAKE

So you have 10 minutes to play and 4 hours to chill. Actually I cheated, an hour and a half in the deep-freeze worked. This is the adult version of the uncooked wonder that any eejit can make. The version we remember from our youth was cooking chocolate, grim glacé cherries and digestives. Try good chocolate, Morello cherries, amaretti morbidi soaked in kirsch, Marcona almonds.

You have NO idea quite how good this artless black block of beatitude is, really you don't. Do not be snobby about its child-like genetic inheritance. This is irresistible.

serves 8–10

200g good-quality dark chocolate (about 70% cocoa solids) (I use Green and Black's)
1 heaped tbsp golden syrup
120g unsalted butter
1 egg, beaten
90g amaretti (ideally morbidi), or digestives or gingernuts will do
1 tsp kirsch, or a little more to taste
50g Marcona almonds, coarsely chopped
50g walnuts, coarsely broken
25g shelled pistachio nuts, coarsely chopped
50g Morello cherries from a jar, drained of syrup, halved

Line a 900g loaf tin with foil or greaseproof paper. Melt the chocolate, golden syrup and butter together gently in a heatproof bowl set over a pan of barely simmering water. Stir to combine and then take off the heat. Let cool slightly, then stir in the beaten egg.

Break the amaretti into large chunks, place in a bowl and sprinkle over the kirsch. Throw in the chopped almonds, walnuts, pistachios and cherries. Pour the warm chocolate mixture over, stir gently until evenly mixed and then pour into the loaf tin.

Place in the fridge for 4 hours to set (or longer if you want to make it earlier). Or cheat – as I did – and whack it in the freezer for 30 minutes.

When you want to eat your superior fridge cake, remove from the fridge and turn it out onto a board. Peel off the foil or paper and cut the cake into thin slices, using a sharp knife. I like it with cream or crème fraîche. Red berries or cherries or a mixture on the side are also good with it.

CHOCOLATE, FIG & WALNUT LOG

Edible presents are always top of my list. Last Christmas, I had a whole gang of children over to make some edible presents for their families. Dense, dark, fruity and cinnamony within, this little log was the most delectable of them all.

It takes minutes to make and seconds to devour. Measure everything in a large cup or a mug for ease and speed.

makes 2 logs

1 cup broken up or roughly chopped dark chocolate (64–72% cocoa solids)
2 cups dried chopped figs
1 cup organic dried apricots or prunes, chopped
1 cup pitted Medjool dates, chopped
1½ tsp ground cinnamon
1 tsp natural vanilla extract
1 cup walnut halves, coarsely chopped
½ cup blanched Marcona (or other good almonds), coarsely chopped
1 cup unrefined icing sugar, sifted, for dredging

Place the chocolate, figs, apricots or prunes, dates, cinnamon and vanilla in a food processor and process to a thick paste. Transfer to a bowl and stir in the chopped walnuts and almonds. Divide the mixture in two.

Dredge your surface generously with icing sugar and place one portion of the mixture in the middle. Sprinkle the paste with more icing sugar and roll into a cylinder, keeping your hands well coated with icing sugar to stop the paste from sticking to them. The log will absorb a lot of icing sugar. Wrap in cling film or cellophane and secure the ends. Repeat to make a second log. Refrigerate until needed.

Either tie the cellophane-wrapped logs with ribbons and give them away as presents, or unwrap and slice to serve. As the logs will absorb icing sugar in the fridge, you may wish to sprinkle a little more over as you unwrap them.

BITTER CHOCOLATE & SALTED CARAMEL BROWNIE CAKE

What a wonderful, cold, dank, dark, wet Saturday afternoon experiment this was. The little crunchy bits of caramel and salt crystals meet your mouth with a sort of explosive surprise. The tender chocolate brownie, as dark and dank as the day, is even better kept in the fridge to eat cold with crème fraîche – the lactic sharpness cuts the rich, sweet goo with aplomb.

serves 10–12

100g unsalted butter
150g dark chocolate (64–72% cocoa solids), broken up
1 large egg
110g light muscovado sugar
1 tsp natural vanilla extract
210g plain flour

for the salted caramel
120g vanilla caster sugar (see page 105)
150ml double cream (ideally Jersey)
scant 1 tsp sea salt crystals

First, make the salted caramel. Warm a heavy-bottomed wide frying pan over a low heat and then scatter the vanilla sugar in an even layer over the base. Leave it to melt and bronze over a low heat. It will probably do so unevenly, but refrain from stirring; instead tilt the pan to slosh the sugar around a bit until it is all molten, mahogany coloured and bubbling gently; do not allow it to burn.

As soon as the caramel is dark and bubbling, carefully pour in the cream (it will splutter) and stir over the heat for a couple of minutes to amalgamate thoroughly. If any big lumps form, stir over the heat until they melt; leave small crunchy bits – these give texture to the finished cake. Remove from the heat and sprinkle over the salt crystals. Pour onto a silicone liner or tray lined with non-stick baking paper and allow to cool and firm up a little while you prepare the cake mixture.

Preheat the oven to 170°C/Gas 3 and put a baking sheet on the middle shelf to heat up. Grease a 23cm springform cake tin, line with non-stick baking paper and butter the paper too.

Put the butter and chocolate into a heatproof bowl and place over a pan of barely simmering water, making sure the bowl is not touching the water, until melted. Lift off the bowl and set aside.

In another bowl, whisk the egg, sugar and vanilla extract together just until evenly combined. Fold in the warm chocolate mixture. Sift the flour over the surface and fold in carefully with a spatula or large metal spoon. Pour the brownie mixture into the prepared tin. Spoon the caramel bit by bit over the surface, gently folding it in with a knife to distribute evenly.

Bake on the hot baking sheet in the middle of the oven and check after 25 minutes by inserting a skewer into the middle. You are looking for a gooey crumb on the skewer. If the mixture looks raw, bake for another 5 minutes.

When ready, place the tin on a wire rack and leave to cool, then chill for a couple of hours or until you want to eat it. Carefully unmould onto a large plate and serve cold, with crème fraîche.

KILLER BLACK & WHITE CHOCOLATE & RASPBERRY CAKE

The truth always lies on the plate. Invite people to try a new cake, saying, 'Be honest, what do you really think?' and the plate will say it all. Not a crumb unpressed to the finger. My son Harry called it the Bruce Bogtrotter of cakes. Why? 'It is really rich and really good, but do you remember how, in the story, he was forced to eat the whole cake? He couldn't do it with this one!' I dare you. (*Also illustrated overleaf*)

makes one deep 20cm cake

75g blanched Marcona almonds
75g skinned hazelnuts
225g dark chocolate (64–72% cocoa solids), broken up
4 eggs, separated
175g vanilla caster sugar (see page 105)

for the filling
200ml crème fraîche
100g good white chocolate, broken up
125g raspberries

for the dark chocolate fondant
60g dark chocolate
3 tbsp double cream

Preheat the oven to 170°C/Gas 3. Butter two 20cm loose-bottomed cake tins. Finely grind the almonds and hazelnuts in a blender or food processor; set aside.

Melt the chocolate in a heatproof bowl over a pan of barely simmering water, making sure the bowl is not touching the water.

Meanwhile, using an electric mixer, whisk the egg yolks with half of the sugar until pale, airy and doubled in volume.

In another large clean bowl, whisk the egg whites until they hold peaks, then gradually whisk in the remaining sugar until it is all incorporated and you have a satiny, softly peaking meringue.

Add half the meringue to the whisked egg yolk mixture and fold in lightly. Pour in the melted chocolate and carefully fold in, followed by the rest of the meringue and finally the ground nuts.

Scrape the mixture into the prepared tins and stand them on a baking tray. Bake in the middle of the oven for 25–30 minutes, until a skewer inserted into the middle comes out clean. Place the tins on a wire rack and leave the cakes to cool.

For the filling, heat the crème fraîche in a small pan just to scalding point, then remove from the heat and stir in the white chocolate. Continue to stir until melted and smooth. Allow to cool, then chill to firm up slightly, to a thick pouring consistency.

Unmould the cakes and place one on a large plate. Pour on the white chocolate mixture and scatter the raspberries on top. Sandwich together with the other cake.

For the dark chocolate fondant, warm the dark chocolate with the cream in a heatproof bowl over a pan of simmering water until melted and smooth. Allow to cool until thickened to a spreading consistency, then pour on top of the cake and spread evenly using a rubber spatula. Allow to set before you indulge…

FEASTS

I celebrate every supper, but a feast is different. It is a statement. It is the big picture. When you paint it you are creating memories, celebrating an event, defining a moment, so your food has to reflect that, but it must not leave you pole-axed with exhaustion and resentment. Ambition is the enemy of the party – vaulting ambition, that is. Know your limitations and exploit them, enjoy them, enjoy the whole shebang, from planning to purchasing to partying. Be brave. Be simple. Be bountiful.

Here are my three key feasts – excluding Christmas – that come round every year in my house, and it all depends on the dependents – my children – and the guests, as to who and how much help I can beg, borrow and cajole.

Remember, if the preparation isn't fun, the party won't be. This is not an ordeal, it is a feast. A feast for the eyes, a feast for the palate, a feast fit for kings, queens, knaves, friends, family. A feast to remember.

MOTHER'S DAY

Mother's day lunch, if you, the mother, are making it for your family, should be about what you want to cook and what you want to eat. It is your present to yourself, a way of celebrating one of the great joys of motherhood, cooking for your family and inspiring your children to do the same. So if they want to help or join in, let them peel, scrub, chop, wash up, and perhaps even make the pud. This passion fruit posset is simple, child-proof, divine. Its sharpness cuts the sweetness of the lamb and the creamy depths of the Romano peppers.

MOTHER'S DAY LUNCH FOR 6

Slow-roasted Spiced Shoulder of Lamb

Flamed Romano Peppers in a Cream Sauce

Umbrian Lentils with Sherry Vinegar

Jasmine Rice with Leeks

Passion Fruit Posset

SLOW-ROASTED SPICED SHOULDER OF LAMB

Those of us who tinker with food for a living inevitably work, re-work, leave and come back to a dish we've created time and time again. This dish evolved from the one on page 88, but I needed a 7-hour reconnaissance with heat, dusky herb and spice for these shoulders of lamb, so we could go walking in the hills and out for a drink without the stress of the timer or the fear of coming home to the scent of something burning or over-cooked.

serves 6

2 half-shoulders of lamb on the bone, about 1.2kg each

for the spice paste
1 heaped tsp smoked paprika
1 tsp ground turmeric
2 tsp cumin seeds, toasted in a dry pan and crushed
½ tsp ground cinnamon
8 black peppercorns
1 large garlic clove, peeled and crushed
½ tsp coarse sea salt
1–2 tbsp olive oil

Preheat the oven to 120°C/Gas ½. Put all the ingredients for the spice paste into a mortar and pound with the pestle to a paste, adding the extra olive oil if the mixture is quite dry.

Make little nicks in the lamb fat all over, using the point of a small, sharp knife. Rub the surface of the lamb with the spice paste, pushing it down into the slits as well as you can. Rub the flesh side, with the paste too.

Put the two half-shoulders, fat side down, into a large, heavy-bottomed cooking pot or flameproof casserole and place over a fairly high heat for 5 minutes or so, until the fat begins to crisp and run.

Turn the meat over, add a cupful of water and bring to the boil. Put the lid on and transfer to the oven. Cook for 6–7 hours, until the meat is meltingly tender and easily pulled from the bone. I check the meat and turn it over every couple of hours, but this isn't essential if you are not around to do so. There will be a lot of lovely spicy liquor at the end of the cooking time. Leave the meat to rest in the pot for 10–15 minutes before serving.

To serve, transfer the lamb to a warmed serving plate. Skim the excess fat from the cooking liquor and reheat if necessary. Simply pull the meat from the bone in soft chunks and serve with the juices spooned over and accompanied by the peppers, lentils and rice.

FLAMED ROMANO PEPPERS IN A CREAM SAUCE

You can prepare these ahead, ready to warm through to serve. Grill 6 Romano (or other) red peppers or scorch by turning on a fork over a gas flame, until charred on all sides. Put into a bowl, cover with cling film and leave for 20 minutes. Peel away the skins, halve the peppers lengthways and remove the seeds, then place all but 2 halves in a small gratin dish with any juices.

Warm 2 tsp olive oil in a saucepan and add a crushed garlic clove and 3–4 chopped thyme sprigs. Cook gently to soften the garlic and scent the oil, but don't let the garlic brown. Add 4 tbsp double cream, bring to the boil, then remove from the heat and season with salt and pepper to taste. Pour into a blender, add the reserved 2 pepper halves and blitz to a pink cream. Taste and adjust the seasoning. Pour over the flamed peppers in the gratin dish.

Just before serving, warm through gently in the oven.

UMBRIAN LENTILS WITH SHERRY VINEGAR

Cook a 450g packet of Umbrian lentils in water according to the packet instructions until just soft, but holding their shape. Remove from the heat and stir in a crushed garlic clove, 1 tsp each chopped coriander and parsley and 3 tbsp each sherry vinegar and olive oil. Season with salt and pepper to taste and adjust before serving.

Any leftover lentils will be delicious dressed with a little more sherry vinegar, olive oil and freshly chopped herbs, and eaten as a salad.

JASMINE RICE WITH LEEKS

Sauté 4 cleaned, chopped leeks in a knob of butter until nearly soft. Meanwhile, start cooking a 450g packet of brown or white jasmine rice in chicken stock or water according to the packet instructions. After 10 minutes, tip in the buttery leeks and continue to cook until the rice is tender.

PASSION FRUIT POSSET

One of those rare occasions when from the gleam in the eye to the finished dish is almost as instant as alchemy. The thing to watch is the lemon. Don't let it intrude, let it counterbalance the sharp, fragrant strength and purity of the passion fruit. Nothing could be simpler to make, yet appear so sumptuous and complex in the mouth. Take the credit. No one will believe your cries of how easy it was to make, they'll think you're being disingenuous.

serves 6

5 passion fruit
450ml thick Jersey or other double cream
110g unrefined caster sugar
juice of 1–1½ large Sicilian lemons, strained

to serve (optional)
citrus amaretti (see page 124) or ricciarelli (see page 125)

Halve the passion fruit, extract 2 tsp of the seeds and reserve for serving. Scoop out the rest of the passion fruit flesh into a sieve set over a bowl and press the pulp in the sieve with the back of a wooden spoon to extract as much juice as possible; discard the pulp. Set aside the juice.

Gently heat the cream and sugar in a saucepan until the sugar is dissolved, then bring to the boil and let bubble for 3 minutes. Remove from the heat. Stir in the juice of ¾ lemon, followed by the passion fruit juice. Taste and add as much more of the lemon juice as you feel the posset needs, keeping the taste firmly in the passion fruit camp.

Pour the mixture into 6 glasses and allow to cool, then refrigerate for 4–6 hours before serving. Finish each posset with a teaspoon-tip of the reserved passion fruit seeds before serving.

MY BIRTHDAY

September. The perfect month for late summer vegetables; tiny yellow and green courgettes with their flowers still attached, vermilion tomatoes ripening on my windowsill, and there are still raspberries in my fruit cage in the garden which should last until November.

I'm cooking my birthday dinner, a feast for 14. Now some people would baulk at the idea, but Miranda, daughter no. 1, has invited everyone and I am going to 'faites' gloriously 'simple' as Carême almost said.

I will make the ice cream a few days ahead and chill the figs in raspberry sauce in the afternoon. The antipasti can be made in a leisurely fashion, followed by the pasta sauce, to be heated through when we cook the pappardelle.

This kind of dinner is not about showing off or being ambitious, it's about the finest ingredients cooked simply, shared with my favourite people in the world. My kind of party.

I've scaled it all down to 6 people for you, but alter it to suit your own number.

BIRTHDAY MENU FOR 6

Baby Courgette Salad with Toasted Pine Nuts

Insalata Tricolore

Egg Pappardelle with a Crimini Mushroom & Marsala Sauce

Chilled Figs in Raspberry Sauce

with Hazelnut Ice Cream

BABY COURGETTE SALAD WITH TOASTED PINE NUTS

Served together with the tricolore, this dish goes way beyond the sum of its individual parts. Try to find some baby-fingered courgettes and a combination of yellow and green if you can to splash the primary palette of these two dishes with more colour. Best at room temperature. (*Illustrated on previous page*)

Serves 6

650g or so small courgettes (ideally mixed yellow and green ones, with flowers attached)
2 tbsp robustly flavoured olive oil
sea salt and black pepper
1 large garlic clove, peeled and finely sliced
finely grated zest of 1 lemon
1 tbsp lemon juice, or to taste
1 tbsp chopped summer savory or 2 tsp chopped thyme leaves
large handful of pine nuts

Trim the bottoms off the courgettes. Keep tiny baby ones whole; if they are a little larger, split them in half lengthways. Heat a heavy-bottomed frying pan over a lively heat and then add the olive oil. When the oil is hot, throw in the courgettes and add a sprinkling of salt. Cook, turning after a few minutes. At this point, they should still be resistant to a knife point. Add the sliced garlic, lower the heat and continue to cook until the courgettes are *al dente*, with some a little softer than others.

Add the lemon zest and juice, and take the pan off the heat. Season with pepper, then taste and adjust, as necessary, adding a little more lemon juice if you think it is needed. Add the chopped herbs and leave to cool to room temperature.

Meanwhile, toast the pine nuts in a hot, dry small frying pan until lightly coloured and beginning to turn oily, shaking them around in the pan. Tip the nuts over the courgettes while still hot. Taste the dish again before heaping it onto the plates, as you may wish to adjust the herbs, seasoning, lemon juice or olive oil at this point.

INSALATA TRICOLORE

A tricolore is dependent on the quality of the ingredients and that alone. Buy the ripest, fullest flavoured tomatoes you can lay your hands on and mozzarella di bufala di campana or burrata, if you can find it and want something even creamier. A grassy, peppery olive oil like the lovely Ravida for your dressing and a genuine, aged balsamic vinegar – there are imposters! And tear rather than slice the mozzarella, the informality feels right on the plate.

Serves 6

500g perfectly ripe, little vine-ripened tomatoes, such as datterini or cherry tomatoes
3 x 250g balls of buffalo mozzarella or burrata (at room temperature)
1 small avocado
spritz of lemon juice
sea salt and black pepper
good, peppery olive oil, to taste
a few drops of aged balsamic vinegar
handful of basil leaves

Halve the tomatoes, tear the mozzarella or burrata and combine on the plate. Halve, stone, peel and slice the avocado and toss in a little lemon juice, then add to the salad. Season with salt and scrunch over some pepper.

Just before serving, dress the salad lightly with olive oil and balsamic vinegar and scatter over the basil leaves. Taste and adjust the seasoning, olive oil and balsamic vinegar as necessary.

EGG PAPPARDELLE WITH A CRIMINI MUSHROOM & MARSALA SAUCE

Crimini mushrooms are meaty and earthy and firmer-textured than ordinary white mushrooms. The Italians also call them 'Roman' or 'brown' mushrooms. If you can't lay your hands on them, chestnut mushrooms will do fine. I think the sage adds muskiness to the earthiness of the 'shrooms, the Marsala sweetness and depth, the crème fraîche a note of lactic sharpness. It is like building up layers of flavours out of a few dissimilar yet complementary ingredients, a complete palette in one dish but a joyously simple and harmonious one. A mixture of half pecorino, half Parmesan grated on top makes this a king of dishes. Make the sauce a few hours in advance and it will be all the better for it.

Serves 6

650g crimini mushrooms, trimmed and wiped clean
18–24 sage leaves, depending on size
30g butter, plus a knob to finish the pasta
2 tbsp olive oil
1 shallot or small onion, peeled and finely sliced
1 large garlic clove, peeled and finely sliced
sea salt and black pepper
150ml dry Marsala
2 heaped tbsp crème fraîche
650g fresh egg pappardelle, or 500g good-quality dried pappardelle (such as Rustichella d'Abruzzo)
50–60g each pecorino and Parmesan, or all Parmesan, freshly grated

Slice the mushrooms and stalks, but not too thinly. Roll up the sage leaves together and slice into slim strips; keep in a separate pile. Heat the butter and all but 2 tsp of the olive oil in a heavy-bottomed frying pan. Throw in the shallot, garlic and mushrooms together and sprinkle over some salt. Cook over a high heat, turning frequently, until the mushrooms begin to exude their juices, then you can slow the heat down a little.

Meanwhile, heat the remaining olive oil in a small frying pan until smoky-hot. Throw in the sage leaves and frazzle them briefly on both sides for a minute or two until crisp. Tip onto a plate.

Once the mushroom juices are flowing, add the Marsala and let it bubble to reduce a little. Continue to cook until the alcohol has burnt off and the mushrooms have softened. At this point, add the crème fraîche, frazzled sage and some pepper. Let bubble together for a minute, then taste and adjust the seasoning, possibly adding a splash more Marsala. The sauce is now ready, so either turn into the pasta immediately or set aside, ready to reheat gently to serve.

When ready to serve, bring a large pot of salted water to a rolling boil. Add the pasta and cook until *al dente*: fresh egg pappardelle takes about 2 minutes; for dried pappardelle refer to the packet directions.

Drain the pappardelle, holding back a little of the cooking water in the pan, and return the pasta to the pan. Add the warm sauce, together with a knob of butter, and half of the cheese. Toss together over the heat for a minute before serving to amalgamate.

Divide between warm pasta bowls and serve at once, with the rest of the cheese in a bowl on the side for guests to help themselves.

CHILLED FIGS IN RASPBERRY SAUCE WITH HAZELNUT ICE CREAM

Figs, raspberries and hazelnuts are natural partners. This fruit is best prepared 4–6 hours ahead to allow time for the figs to absorb the raspberry sauce. Make the ice cream a day or two in advance – these quantities are generous, so you should have some for the next day. Or, you could serve the figs with crème fraîche with a little Cointreau whisked in, or with thick yoghurt and a little acacia honey trickled over. (*Illustrated on following page*)

Serves 6

12 figs
350g raspberries
1–2 tbsp unrefined icing sugar, to taste, sifted
a spritz of lemon juice

for the hazelnut ice cream
250g hazelnuts (in their skins)
180g vanilla caster sugar (see page 105)
500ml whole milk (ideally Jersey)
250ml Jersey or other rich double cream
6 large egg yolks

First make the ice cream. Preheat the oven to 200°C/Gas 6. Scatter the hazelnuts on a roasting tray and place in the oven for 5–10 minutes until the skins appear toasted but not burnt. Rub the nuts in a tea towel to remove the papery skins.

Gently heat 120g of the vanilla caster sugar in a heavy-bottomed frying pan until it melts and begins to colour, swirling the pan around a little to encourage the sugar to dissolve evenly, but don't stir. Allow the sugar to turn a mahogany colour, but no darker or it will become bitter. Immediately add the nuts, stir them around for a few seconds and then tip the mixture onto a buttered baking tray. Leave to cool and harden. Once cooled, break up the praline and whiz in a food processor to a powder and beyond, to almost a paste.

To make the custard, heat the milk and cream in a heavy-bottomed pan to scalding point. Meanwhile, whisk the egg yolks and remaining 60g vanilla sugar together in a large bowl, then slowly pour on the hot creamy milk, whisking as you do so. Pour through a sieve back into the pan and whisk over a low heat until the mixture thickens enough to lightly coat the back of a spoon; don't let it boil otherwise it might curdle. Pour the custard straight into a bowl set over ice to cool, giving it an occasional stir to stop a skin forming on the surface.

Once cooled, stir in the hazelnut praline and churn in the ice-cream maker until thick. Transfer to a suitable container, seal and keep in the freezer. (Best eaten within a few days.)

To prepare the figs, cut them into slices. Whiz the raspberries in a blender or food processor, then pass through a sieve into a bowl to remove the seeds, pressing the pulp in the sieve with the back of a wooden spoon to extract as much juice as possible. Add icing sugar to taste (I like to keep mine tart) and a spritz of lemon juice to bring out the flavour of the raspberries. Layer the sliced figs and raspberry sauce in pretty glass dishes, then cover and chill.

Remove the figs from the fridge 10 minutes before serving. Take out the ice cream at the same time to let it soften slightly. Serve the figs with the hazelnut ice cream.

NEW YEAR'S EVE

On New Year's Eve I cooked this sumptuous Maharaja of a dish for 26. It is over 50 years since the Moti Mahal restaurant in Old Delhi created it and, since then, people all over the world have come to make their own version of what has become known as 'the dish you would sell your soul for'. I made it with a whole, organic turkey, cooked off the bone for party-ease, and served it with dhal, cucumber raita, spicy fried bananas, fragrant basmati rice and mango chutney. If you're making it for 8 go back to the original chicken.

Almost everything was prepared in advance. I had made the trifle a couple of days ahead and left it in the fridge to allow it to mature. On the night, all I had to do was my main course warm-ups. The dinner was done – the Murgh had been cooked the day before and marrying its flavours overnight in the fridge. I made dhal in the afternoon, so there was only the basmati rice and bananas to cook.

It was the most spectacular feast to see out the old and see in the new with, something that eclipsed even the twice-in-two decades blue moon, which we serenaded with its eponymous song round the piano at midnight.

NEW YEAR'S EVE DINNER FOR 8

Murgh Makhanwala (or Butter Chicken)

Fragrant Basmati Rice

Bananas fried with Spices

Cucumber Raita

Spiced Dhal

Patricia's Mango Chutney

Decadent Trifle

MURGH MAKHANWALA

This Maharaja of a dish really wasn't any more time-consuming or demanding to make for 26 than for the 8 here. Don't be hidebound by the recipe, you will know how much chilli you can take, and if you can't find curry leaves just add more spice – a little garam masala here, a little cardamom there. The marinade can be pasted onto the pieces of chicken up to a day ahead of cooking time and left covered in the fridge.

serves 8

1 organic or free-range chicken, about 2.5kg, jointed, or 8 large chicken thighs (or a combination of legs, thighs, breast)

for the marinade

a finger of fresh root ginger, coarsely grated
4 garlic cloves, peeled and sliced
juice of 1 lemon
1 tbsp olive oil
1 red chilli, deseeded and chopped
1 green chilli, deseeded and chopped
1 tsp garam masala
sea salt
4 heaped tbsp live yoghurt, strained

for the sauce

2 x 400g tins plum tomatoes
1 tbsp tomato purée
a finger of fresh root ginger, grated
4 garlic cloves, peeled and chopped
2 tsp sugar
seeds from 6 crushed cardamom pods
1 scant tsp dried chilli flakes
2 bay leaves
2 green chillies, deseeded and halved lengthways
4 dried curry leaves
2 cloves and 4 allspice, crushed together
1 tsp garam masala
60g unsalted butter, diced
4 tbsp single cream
sea salt and black pepper

to finish

handful of parsley leaves, chopped
a little extra grated fresh root ginger (optional)

Remove the skin from the chicken pieces and slash the flesh on the diagonal with the point of a knife in a few places. Place in a large baking dish. Whiz all the ingredients for the marinade, except the yoghurt, in a food processor to a slushy, but textured paste. Stir in the yoghurt and pour the marinade over the chicken, rubbing it into the slashes. Cover and leave to marinate in a cool place for at least an hour or overnight in the fridge.

Remove the dish from the fridge an hour before cooking to bring it to room temperature. Preheat the oven to 200°C/Gas 6.

Bake the chicken for 20 minutes, turning halfway through. It will only be partially cooked at this stage.

In the meantime, prepare the sauce. Plop the tomatoes into a wide heavy-bottomed frying pan and cut them up over the heat, then add the tomato purée, ginger, garlic, sugar, cardamom seeds, chilli flakes and bay leaves. Cover and simmer for 20 minutes, then fish out the bay and either blitz in a blender or push through the coarse disc of a mouli (food mill), my preferred method for texture.

Return the sauce to the pan and sprinkle over the green chillies, curry leaves and crushed cloves and allspice. Immerse the chicken pieces in the sauce, adding their marinade. Sprinkle over the garam masala and simmer for a further 15 minutes or until the chicken is cooked through. To test, pierce the thickest part of a thigh with a skewer; the juices should run clear.

Stir the diced butter into the sauce, followed by the cream. Season with salt and pepper to taste. Remove from the heat and leave to stand, covered, for 5 minutes.

To serve, sprinkle with a little chopped parsley and, if you like, a little extra grated root ginger. Everyone needs lots of sauce to soak into the basmati rice underneath.

FRAGRANT BASMATI RICE

Allow 450g brown basmati rice for 8 people. Before you start to cook the rice, put a handful of raisins to soak in a little warm water. Heat 1 tbsp oil in a medium saucepan, then add the rice and stir around for a minute. Sprinkle with 1 heaped tsp ground turmeric and 6 lightly crushed cardamom pods, then pour in enough water to come 1cm over the top of the rice. Bring to the boil, lower the heat and simmer with the lid on. After about 15 minutes, check that the water hasn't all been absorbed, adding a little more if it seems too dry. Re-cover and continue to cook until *al dente.* Meanwhile, toast a handful of flaked almonds in a small pan until biscuity coloured and slightly oily. Drain the raisins and fork through the rice with the toasted almonds, a knob of butter and 1 tbsp chopped coriander leaves, if you wish. Serve hot.

BANANAS FRIED WITH SPICES

Use firm bananas – greener rather than ripe, as they won't break down as readily on cooking. Allow ½ banana per person. Cut the bananas into slices on the slant. Toast 1 tsp kalonji (nigella) seeds and ½ tsp cardamom seeds (from crushed pods) in a dry pan until they begin to pop and smell toasty. Add 1 tbsp mild-flavoured oil, such as groundnut or light olive. When hot, add the bananas and cook for a couple of minutes on one side, then turn them gently, coating them in the seeds. Cook on the other side for a minute or two, then turn into a bowl and sprinkle over a little lime or lemon juice. Serve warm.

CUCUMBER RAITA

Drain a 500g carton of Greek yoghurt in a muslin-lined sieve for half an hour and then plop it into a serving bowl. Peel ½ cucumber, split lengthways and scoop out the seeds, then dice finely and drain on kitchen paper. Add the cucumber to the yoghurt with a crushed garlic clove, a sprinkling of salt, a scrunch of black pepper and 1 tsp toasted and crushed cumin seeds. Stir, then taste and adjust the seasoning and spice if you need to. Refrigerate until needed. Just before serving, if you have some fresh mint to hand, stir 1 tsp finely shredded leaves through the raita and sprinkle the same amount over the top.

SPICED DHAL

serves 8–10 (as a side dish)

400g packet urad dhal or red lentils
2½ tbsp olive oil
1 tsp ground turmeric
½ cinnamon stick
2 cloves
a finger of fresh root ginger, peeled and sliced
4 cardamom pods, lightly crushed
bunch of coriander, stalks and leaves separated and chopped
1 green chilli, deseeded and sliced
1 garlic clove, peeled
1 small onion, peeled and finely sliced
1 tsp garam masala
1–2 tsp cumin seeds, toasted in a dry pan and ground
sea salt
1 tbsp roughly chopped coriander leaves

Wash the dhal or lentils, tip into a large, heavy-bottomed cooking pot or pan and sprinkle 2 tbsp olive oil over the surface. Cook, stirring, over a medium heat to coat the pulses in the oil (as you would risotto rice). Sprinkle over the turmeric, then add enough cold water to cover by 1cm or so. Add the cinnamon, cloves, ginger, cardamom pods, chopped coriander stalks, chilli and whole garlic clove. Bring slowly to the boil, then skim off any froth from the surface.

Cover and simmer for about 40 minutes until tender, checking halfway through cooking to see if the dhal has absorbed all the water, and topping up if you need to. The dish should end up quite sloppy, so keep checking towards the end of cooking. Remove the garlic, cloves, cardamom pods and chunky bits of cinnamon and ginger if you can catch them.

Meanwhile, heat the remaining olive oil in a frying pan. When hot, add the sliced onion and immediately sprinkle with the garam masala. Fry, stirring, until softened, browned and starting to crisp. Now stir in ½ tsp toasted cumin and remove from the heat.

Before serving, season with salt and add more toasted cumin to taste. Transfer to a warmed serving bowl, scatter over the browned onion and chopped coriander leaves and it's ready.

PATRICIA'S MANGO CHUTNEY

makes 5 x 375g jars

6 ripe, firm mangoes
2 tbsp vegetable oil
1 tbsp black mustard seeds
½ tsp cardamom seeds
1½ tbsp cumin seeds
2 medium onions, peeled and chopped
2 red chillies, deseeded for less heat if preferred, chopped
5 garlic cloves, peeled and crushed
1 tbsp freshly grated root ginger
1½ tbsp ground coriander
3 tsp ground turmeric
280g caster sugar
2 tsp salt
250ml white wine vinegar
125ml malt vinegar

Cut the mangoes either side of the stone, then peel and chop the flesh into 2–3cm pieces. Set aside.

Heat the oil in a heavy-bottomed wide saucepan and cook the mustard, cardamom and cumin seeds for about a minute until they pop and release their fragrance. Add the onions, chillies, garlic and ginger and cook until soft and lightly browned. Stir in the ground spices and cook until fragrant.

Add the chopped mangoes, sugar, salt and vinegars. Bring to the boil, lower the heat and simmer, uncovered, for 1–1½ hours until thickened, stirring occasionally. Pour the chutney into sterilised jars while still hot, and cover.

Keep for a couple of months before eating... if you can resist.

DECADENT TRIFLE

My son Harry christened this epicurean Golgotha of a trifle after he had tasted it and I couldn't think how, adequately, to describe it. A thing of such beauteous hidden depths and layers of flavour that I swoon to think of it. If you want to cut a corner, buy a ginger cake, and don't bother with the miniature white chocolate snowballs – simply scatter fresh berries and shaved chocolate on top.

serves 10

for the ginger cake base
120g unsalted butter, softened
50g molasses sugar
50g light muscovado sugar
2 eggs
2 heaped tbsp blackstrap molasses
225g self-raising flour
1½ tsp ground ginger
5 balls of preserved stem ginger, finely chopped, plus 2 tbsp of the syrup from the jar
½ tsp bicarbonate of soda
2 tbsp tepid milk
large handful of cranberries (optional)
2 tbsp Oloroso sherry, for sprinkling

for the custard and fruit
90g dark chocolate (70% cocoa solids)
90g good white chocolate
2 eggs, plus 2 egg yolks
1 heaped tbsp rice flour
1 tbsp vanilla caster sugar (see page 105)
600ml single cream
250g raspberries
2 tbsp kirsch
150g blueberries
170g (½ jar) good raspberry jam

for the syllabub
grated zest and juice of 1 large lemon
1 tbsp Oloroso sherry
1 tbsp Cognac
50g vanilla caster sugar (see page 105)
300ml double cream (ideally Jersey)

to decorate
30g white chocolate
15g unsalted butter
handful of mixed blueberries and cranberries

For the cake base, preheat the oven to 170°C/Gas 3. Line a 23 x 12cm loaf tin with non-stick baking paper. Using an electric mixer, cream the butter and sugars together thoroughly, then beat in the eggs one at a time, followed by the molasses. Sift in the flour and ground ginger and fold in, together with the chopped stem ginger and syrup. Dissolve the bicarbonate of soda in the milk and fold through the cake mixture with the cranberries, if using. Turn into the prepared loaf tin and bake for about 1 hour, testing with a skewer after 50 minutes.

Leave the cake to cool in the tin on a wire rack for 30 minutes, then turn out and leave to cool completely. You will need about a third of the cake for the trifle. Wrapped in foil in a tin, the rest will stay delectably sticky for up to a week.

Slice a third of the cake, arrange in a large glass serving bowl and sprinkle with the sherry. Set aside.

To make the custard, break both chocolates into pieces and place in separate bowls. Beat the whole eggs, egg yolks, rice flour and sugar together. Heat the cream to scalding point and then pour it onto the eggs, whisking as you go. Return to the pan and whisk over a gentle heat until thickened. Pour half the custard onto the dark chocolate, whisking constantly until melted and smooth. Do similarly with the white chocolate.

Pour the dark custard over the trifle base and leave to cool and set, then scatter over the raspberries and sprinkle with the kirsch. Fold the blueberries into the white chocolate custard, pour over the raspberries and leave to set.

Melt the raspberry jam with 1 tbsp water and pour over the set white custard.

To make the syllabub, combine the lemon zest and juice, sherry and Cognac in a large bowl, add the sugar and stir until dissolved. Pour in the cream and beat gently until the mixture holds its shape in soft billows. Spoon the syllabub evenly onto the trifle.

For the decoration, melt the white chocolate with the butter in a heatproof bowl over a pan of simmering water, then take off the heat. One at a time, spear each berry onto a cocktail stick, dip into the warm chocolate and turn to coat, then lay on a sheet of lightly oiled foil and leave until set. Leave some of the berries uncoated.

Stud the trifle with the berries in your own decorative way. Refrigerate until ready to serve.

INDEX

D

E

F

N

O

P

ACKNOWLEDGEMENTS

In no particular order, as they say in so many competitions that shall remain nameless:
Daughter no.1 Miranda For being the eyes and the palate and pen and helper on the shooting of all the recipes. If she can cook these dishes from my instructions without adding her pencil-marks and questions, so can you. **Simon Wheeler** How lovely to work together again, which we hadn't done since my very first book, all of 15 years ago. The perfectionist par excellence, not a detail escapes him and his eye is unrivalled. **Lucy Gowans** Patient, precise, the interpreter of the look, the feel, the taste, the smell of this book. And her daughters loved all the cakes. **Jane O'Shea** Whose taste and judgement and measure and enthusiasm allow me to create these pages, these dishes, this book. **Helen Lewis** Who is simply a design dream. Her ideas are always on the button. **Alison Cathie** Who has invited me back to partner her in a further dance at Quadrille.